Poggioreale of Sicily From Peasant Civilization to Today

An English translation of the
Erasmo Vella Book,
*Poggioreale di Sicilia
tra civiltà contadina
e odierna società, 2003*

By
Christine R. Anderson and Ross Todaro, Jr.
Co-Founders of Poggioreale in America Inc.
Second in a Series

Poggioreale
—IN AMERICA—

Copyright © 2023 by
Christine R. Anderson and Ross Todaro, Jr.
Co-Founders
Poggioreale in America Inc.

All rights reserved.
No part of this book may be produced
or used in any manner without written permission
of the copyright owner except for
the use of quotations in a book review.

First hardback edition May 2023

Book cover design by Anne Boykin.
Cover Photo by Kathlyn Dragna.
Translation of the Vella Book
was commissioned by Poggioreale in America,
thank you for your work, Sarah Schneider, CT.
Special appreciation to Rosario Sanfilippo
for graciously helping with Sicilian passages.

ISBN 979-8-218-11873-0

We are on this journey together,
you and I, and together we are getting to know
our ancestors from Poggioreale.
As we learn about their stories and culture,
we can almost hear our ancestors telling us
who and why they were
... and we realize
that along the way ...
we are getting to know ourselves.

Ackowledgements

We thank our family, friends and Poggioreale in America colleagues on three continents for cheering us on! This writing project has brought multiple familes together for one purpose.

Texas: Marilyn Maniscalco Henley has been with us for a long time and still hasn't grown tired of us, thankfully. Anne Boykin is always there to advise and to enhance so many of our efforts. Kathlyn Dragna listens, helps and then gives us gorgeous photography to share with our readers.

California: Sarah Campise Hallier joined us in our obsession and has given us a great deal of time and leadership. Sarah Schneider has become more than our translator; she is our literary and language teacher and companion, always at the ready.

Sicily: Giocchino Coco is a secret weapon for research and accuracy in our quest for Poggioreale information. Mimmo Cangelosi has been a constant supporter and patient helper. Rosario Sanfillipo is a dedicated researcher and friend, and provides invaluable assistance, always. And most of all our cousin, Anna Todaro; how lucky for us that we found such an talented and loving cousin who is always offering her generous help!

Australia: Lina Maiorana, a font of Poggiorealese wisdom and info, introduced us to our extended community in Australia. Nunzio Anthony Pace made our quest to know his Uncle Erasmo come true, and obtained his biography so we could present some highlights of his life accomplishments in this book.

We are pleased to continue our mission to increase our virtual library so we can share with you, our global *paesani*.

Contents

Introduction:
    Learning about Poggioreale   9
    Modern Books by Poggiorealese Authors   10
    Historical Books about Poggioreale   11
    Meet Professor Erasmo Vella   13
    Other Vella Publications   18

Our Translation of *Poggioreale di Sicilia tra civiltà contadina e odierna società* by Erasmo Vella:
    Translation Begins   22
    Preface by Mario Grasso   23
    List of Chapters, Book Photos   28
    End of Translation   232

Message from the Authors   233

Poggioreale (Trapani) - Madrice e Piazza Elimo
www.poggiorealeinamerica.com

Introduction

Our ancestors came from Poggioreale, Sicly. As kids, we were raised amidst large and lively family gatherings with foods that were *delizioso*, all made by loved ones whose arms were open wide and cheeks poised to receive our kisses. Their voices were almost melodic and sometimes thunderous in their exhuberance. These experiences gave rise to our developing ethnic identity. And in the quiet times, nothing made more of an indelible mark on our souls than sitting on a nonno's lap, rolling dough for *cuccidati* alongside nonna and the "zias," or listening to them exchange stories of their long-ago childhoods on another continent.

Learning about Poggioreale

Like so many of our *paesani*, we didn't think about uncovering our people's history until we were grown with families of our own. Sure, over the years, we heard a few of their immigration tales, and were told why our grandparents or great grandparents left their cherished Sicilian homeland to sail to America. But as we got older, we realized that our immigrant elders neglected to tell us enough! So often we would wonder aloud, "Why didn't I ask more questions when they were still alive?" Surely you, too, have thought the same thing. It might even be the reason you are reading this book.

No doubt you relish the fact that you are of Italian heritage! We do! We chatter, cook and celebrate using both Italian and Sicilian words, eat traditional foods, and use expressions and near-constant hand gestures that our people have used for centuries! But oh, how learning the details of our shared history has brought us an awakening …. and an enhanced cultural understanding. This is why you, too, will enjoy learning about Poggioreale, the village that made your ancestors who and what *they were* … and without a doubt influenced who and what *we are* in the here and now.

As for us, we authors began our family studies in earnest only a handful of years ago. Unlike our elders, we were fortunate to have a means to learn some historical facts about our far-away ancestral town; the internet brought us bits of information and even a few videos to electronically transport us to the site of Poggioreale's ruins in Sicily. Our immigrant ancestors didn't have that luxury; they only could reminisce. As social media developed, opportunities to expand our contacts with other descendants grew, and it was fun to find others with simpatico experiences. It was for this reason we co-founded Poggioreale in America. We are proud to say that our PIA Facebook page, created in 2018, has given us an entertaining and educational platform to connect with others who share our unique heritage. Still, we continued to search for written historical sources. Eventually we discovered that there were published works about Poggioreale, but they were written in Italy … and so we wanted to find them, and then tell everyone about them!

Modern Books by Poggiorealese Authors

We turned our attention to Sicily to look for written materials about Poggioreale. We found that the town had given rise to many passionate and talented authors, and continues to do so! How fortunate for those of us who wish to learn about the people who have inhabited the town over many generations.

For example, we discovered the writings of Giovanni Maniscalco (1935-2015,) a popular mayor who served four terms in office. In 2004 he wrote "Lu due Poggioreale, ieri e oggi" (The Two Poggioreales, Yesterday and Today.) It is a book dedicated to telling the story of the many residents who migrated to Australia. We don't yet have access to an English translation; however, for reference, a copy of his Italian text is currently presented on our website. In 2011, Maniscalco published *"Poggioreale di Sicilia, le famiglie - anni '50 (Poggioreale of Sicily, the families of the 1950s.)* Here he pays tribute to his home town, presents historical notes about its country life, and provides autobiographical experiences. Again, we have not located an English translation, but we look forward to reading and sharing these wonderful books in the future.

We also became aware of the books of Professor Gaetano Zummo (1935-2018) who became a writer and poet in his later years. During his lifetime as a renowned professor, he contributed heavily to the intellectual and artistic environment of Poggioreale and beyond. On our website, poggiorealeinamerica.com, we have presented his impressive personal story along with a summary of his many life accomplishments. A prolific writer, he gave his countrymen four publications in a short period of time: *Rosalia "la Siciliana" (Rosalia "The Sicilian") in* 2012, *Un mondo scomparso (A Vanished World)* in 2015, *Omicidi tra intrigo, trasgressione e mistero (Le indagini su 'la mantide religiousa" e la misteriosa morte del notaio pantaleone) (Murders between Intrigue, Transgresson and Mystery: The Investigations into the Praying Mantis and the Mysterious Death of the Notary Pantaleone") in* 2015 and, finally, his *Petali di stelle, Poesie in lingua e in siciliano* (Petals of the Stars, Poems in the Sicilian Language) in 2018. We would like to bring his works to the English-speaking world, and we look forward to translating them all one day.

Historical Books about Poggioreale

As of this writing, we have found three esteemed authors who published historical books about Poggioreale, Sicily. These publications are many decades apart. Arciprete Nunzio Caronna (1861-1928) was the first to publish in 1901, Can. Dr. Francesco Aloisio (1877-1965) published in 1956, and Professor Erasmo Vella (born in 1928) published in 2003. We were inspired! As students of Poggioreale and beneficiaries of its culture, educational doors were opening to us.

The earliest author, Archiprete Nunzio Caronna, wrote about his birthplace in two books in the early 1900s. He was a cleric and an illustrious son of Poggioreale. His ground-breaking book, *Memorie Storiche di Poggioreale* was published in Sicily in 1901; it was followed by *Vita Civile o supplimento alla monografia storica* in 1906. Both books painted a picture of what life was like in the Sicily of his era, and for our our own grandparents. His books are beautifully written, filled with picturesque images of the Poggioreale of his lifetime. Original copies of these texts are rare; vintage books were nearly impossible to find. Finally, we located digital scans of these two books in a Palermo library, and we quickly commissioned English translations. As a result, Poggioreale in America translated and introduced these two Caronna works to English-speaking descendants in our first book, *Love Letters to Poggioreale*,* published in 2022.

A second important author published a historical book in 1956. Can. Dr. Francesco Aloisio was also a noted cleric and, interestingly, a nephew of Arciprete Caronna. Aloisio's book, *Storia di Poggioreale (Sicilia,)*** is an expanded historical and cultural study of Poggioreale and its people. It quickly became a frequently referenced work by the residents of the town. Sadly, it was virtually unknown on other continents.

Fortunately, a copy of the book was given to a visiting American cousin while he was in Poggioreale. He brought it home to Texas where, in 1995, he and three other cousins shared the cost of having the Aloisio text translated into English in 1999. Two of the cousins privately printed their translated books. For the first time, Americans of Poggiorealese descent were able to read about the history of their family's homeland the way it was prior to the devastating 1968 earthquake. Later this year, an updated and more comprehensive translation of the *Storia di Poggioreale* will be published by Poggioreale in America co-founder & contributor Marilyn Maniscalco Henley and her daughter, Shelly Henley Kelly, C.A. We are looking forward to their book.

A third author in 2003 published a modern review of his home town's history. Professor Erasmo Vella, also a son of Poggioreale, was a professor of literature. His published work, *Poggioreale di Sicilia tra civiltà contadina e ordierna società,* was introduced and enthusiastically received by the residents. Professor Vella's book brings us from Poggioreale Vecchia (Old) to Poggioreale Nuovo (New.) He describes how the residents experienced the earthquake, what their uncomfortable life in temporary housing was like, and the transition to the newly-built town only a few kilometers from the ruins. Bringing his insight to modern times, he discusses the devastating effect of the 1968 earthquake on the residents whose lives were changed forever.

We were given a copy of the Erasmo Vella book by Mayor (*Sindaco*) Mimmo Cangelosi in 2019 when we visited Poggioreale with a group of travelers who shared our ancestry. It was a pilgrimage that was life-changing for us all, and being introduced to Erasmo Vella's book added to the experience. Moreover, it gave us a new opportunity to translate a book that would be of great interest to earnest students of Poggioreale. Once we returned home, we set about the task of commissioning an English translation so we could continue our personal mission.

Meet Professor Erasmo Vella

Professor Erasmo Vella is an accomplished and esteemed son of Poggioreale. He is also the uncle of our friend, Nunzio Anthony Pace of Sydney, Australia, whom we thank for making this biography possible. Born in Poggioreale himself, Nunzio migrated to Australia with his parents to in 1956. He was kind enough to reach out on our behalf to his dear Uncle Erasmo who is ninety-four years old and still resides in Sicily. After a recent visit with his uncle in Palermo, he thanked Professor Vella for us for allowing Poggioreale in America to present his book to the English-speaking *paesani* around the world.

Erasmo Vella was born in Poggioreale on December 29, 1928 to Giuseppe Vella and Giuseppa Cannizzaro. Erasmo spent most of his childhood with his parents on their lands where they owned a water mill. There the grain harvested by the local workers was ground into flour. His father's main goal was to earn money to support the family and to pay for his children's studies. In those days, it was tradition that the children had to carry on the work of their father and provide for the future of the family.

Erasmo says that his best memories were the times spent working with his father at the mill because they allowed him to experience dedication to hard work, but also to enjoy the fruits of their toil. He explains that these times allowed him to experience life's genuine moments despite the hardships of the everyday physical work.

In spite of residing in Palermo now, Erasmo tells us that Poggioreale still occupies his thoughts and holds a special place in his heart. Not only was he born there, he still remembers the days spent in elementary school where his love for literature was born. He attended Poggioreale's elementary school and Alcamo's middle and high school. He then attended the University at Palermo where he obtained a degree in Classical Literature. His activity as a professor began by giving private lessons to young students. His first professorship was in Sardinia. He has taught Italian, Latin and history in high schools in Italy. Even after graduating with his degree from the University of Palermo, he continued to teach Italian at the state schools.

In 1957, Erasmo married a girl from Poggioreale, Dorotea Salvaggio. From the marriage three children were born: Giuseppe, Calogero and Maria Concetta were born in Palermo where the family lives today.

In addition to being a professor of literature, he is also an author. At an early age, Erasmo immersed himself in writing. His pieces centered around life experiences and travel. He has traveled througout Italy as a visitor, and also for his teaching activity as an external member in the Maturity Exam Commissions in various Italian cities. In his maturity his writing focused on travel, romance and antiquity. His writing includes various recollections and hunting stories. He also wrote for the *Encyclopedic Dictionary of Thinkers and Theologians of Sicily Sec XIX and XX, Vol. II* on the Archpriest Nunzio Caronna. He even wrote a love story.

In 2003 Professor Vella published his comprehensive historical piece entitled *Poggioreale di Sicilia tra civiltà contadina e odierna società (Pogioreale of Sicily, from Peasant Civilization to Today)*. This is the work that we proudly present to you here in this, our second book.

His publisher, Prova d'Autore of Palermo, wrote this about Professor Vella on Page 205:

> *"A careful scholar of classical works, he has collaborated with press, publishing essays and research. He has also devoted particular attention to history and in particular to that of Sicily, as is amply demonstrated in this book."*

Professor Vella himself tells us that his work describes the peasant life that once existed in Poggioreale as compared to today's society. In this book he communicates what he calls "the generational and epochal gap that leaves the memory of a simple, tiring but genuine life where the fulcrum is a life rich in traditions."

It is with profound appreciation and respect to Erasmo Vella that we give the world's English-speaking descendants of Poggioreale the rich gift of his wisdom and historical perspective in his in-depth work. He and his family know that we can now share his words with an expanded global family. In this way they, too, can become his newest students.

Christine Rose (Todaro) Anderson
Ross Todaro, Jr.
May 2023

Notes:

Love Letters to Poggioreale, Sicily: A English Translation of Books by Arciprete Nunzio Caronna, 1901-1906. Anderson, Christine R. and Todaro, Ross Jr. Houston, Poggioreale in America Inc, 2022. Available on amazon.

**Storia di Poggioreale (Sicilia).* Aloisio, Can. Dr. Francesco. Palermo, Boccone del Povero. 1956. Please go to our website *poggiorealeinamerica.com* to read about the various editions of this work.

Our Story:
Poggioreale in America and its Facebook Page were established in February, 2018. Our website *poggiorealeinamerica.com* had its Grand Opening on March 19, 2021. We became a Non-Profit organization in 2022, registered in Wisconsin.

Read about Poggioreale in America, our story and mission in our first publication, "Love Letters to Poggioreale" as notated above.

Donations towards our research projects and historical preservation are tax deductible. We invite you to follow our activities and to join our group by signing up on our website.

Looking to learn about YOUR Poggiorealesi ancestors?
Our website can be accessed at
poggiorealeinamerica.com .
Just use the search bar for quick results.

Professor Erasmo Vella
Palermo, 2023

Books Published by Erasmo Vella

In viaggio (In Journey.)
    Vella, Erasmo. Catania, Provo d'Autore, 1999.
Poggioreale di Sicilia tra civiltà contadina e odierna società. (Poggioreale of Sicily, from Peasant Civilization to Today.)
    Vella, Erasmo, Catania, Prova d'Autore, 2003.
Atti del convegno commemorativo sulla figura e le opere dell'Arciprete N. Caronna e del Canonico Dott. Francesco Aloisio.
    Vella, Prof. Erasmo and Ins. Zummo, Gaetano. Catania, Prova d'Autore, 2006.
Una storia d"amore d'altri tempi (A Love Story of Yesteryear.)
    Vella, Erasmo. Catania, Prova d"Autore, 2014.

As of this writing, we don't have details or transcripts
from various speeches or presentations by Erasmo Vella
on various socio-cultural, ethical and/or other professional topics.
Further, we are aware that Professor Vella was an honored presenter
at cultural events held in Poggioreale over the years.
Should our readers have information about these,
or other published works by Vella,
please contact us through our website
as we strive to collect accurate and current information.

*Nunzio Anthony Pace
with his Uncle Erasmo, 2023*

20

Poggioreale of Sicily from Peasant Civilization to Today

Our Translation of

POGGIOREALE DI SICILIA TRA CIVILTÀ CONTADINA E ODIERNA SOCIETÀ
By
Erasmo Vella, 2003

~

Prova d' Autore

Translated for
Poggioreale in America Inc.
2021

------------ Translation Begins ------------

Note:
Our English translation is presented page by page
according to the Italian text.
Original page numbers are referenced
at the botttom of each page (between hypens.)

Preface
By Mario Grasso

Centuries of Civilization

1) We believe that this rich, loving historical report on Poggioreale in Sicily from its municipal origins to the present day, an account that Professor Erasmo Vella wrote using specific and general studies, should immediately be classified as one of the few works that best describes an era and a place. We came to this conclusion thanks to both the specific historical reconstructions placed within the regional and national panorama of at least five centuries of events, and by the calibrated considerations on the recalled facts: true moral reflections which each time synthesize the author's thoughts and illustrate the aspects of events without sparing any severe or nostalgic regrets.

As a scrupulous historian and prudent scholar, Erasmo Vella never lets himself be influenced by appearances; he investigates between documents and written testimonies to discover the hidden meanings, measure the immediate consequences and those that could influence the social, economic, religious, political and, in a single word, moral and civil course of the Poggiorealese municipal community. A community of which Vella remains a grateful son in the name of his ancestors, all of the same lineage with which his own ancestors have shared, over the centuries, many pains and few joys, much work and rare leisure with the proud awareness of those who have never stopped working to build better times for the benefit of future generations.

The intense moments of this historical overview revolve around this fundamental concept.

2) Divided into chapters and embellished with 40 images that allow each reader to figuratively connect with a world of places, people and lived facts, this powerful book by Erasmo Vella reviews and analyzes the *unfolding of life in Poggioreale, referring to each previous bibliography, ordering fragments and references, faithfully interpreting the moral legacies, giving each element described an aura of tangible realism. To obtain these results, the scholar used deductive methods, assembling his accounts into categories to give body to as many analyses of the details: from agricultural crops to religious faith, from work tools to Christmas novenas, from families gathered around a fire pit to the risky nighttime travels of those who once had to walk from Poggioreale to Salaparuta to take a train to Palermo. Vella chooses to add the richness of documented reports and accuracy to the parsimony of savory and demonstrative anecdotes, reconstructing the vocabulary of acts, customary habits, peculiar work, tools, recurrences, up to creating an impeccable encyclopedia on the peasant civilization now inexorably embalmed in the archives of history.*

I speak of the vocabulary reconstructed for each sectoral reference, one of the many demonstrations of Vella's scientific commitment, the results of which ethnology scholars will henceforth be called upon to document.

3) But Vella is not only a historian as shown here by the precision, scrupulousness, and expertise of his complex research, by the surprising and focused deductions he knows how to draw from his work of consultations, comparisons and unprecedented investigations between ancient chronicles and documents scattered in libraries and archives. To this technique and patience of those who are called on to prove themselves notaries of history, Vella adds the exceptional talent of a narrator, the delicacy of a poet, the moral consistency of a citizen who does not hesitate to convey his grievances alongside praise and satisfaction. In fact, the readers of this book will not miss the alarming tensions of the moments in which Vella, after reports on certain political and social developments, stigmatizes his disappointment as a citizen, as pater familias and as an educated scholar with a single sentence, with a clear concept and with calibrated allusiveness. And the more all the brief considerations accompanying the facts recorded are effective, the more they reveal to the reader the spontaneous reaction of a wounded conscience, the emotional participation in the rendering of the facts as they were. And the value of Vella's moral contamination is appreciated every time, precisely because far from becoming parenetic, it tends to accompany revelations of behaviors that do not honor the human and civil character of man with certain and concise stigmatization, whatever the extents or historical moments of a reprehensible gesture. I give the floor to the author for a significant example:

"Giugno, la falce in pugno!" This is the expression used in the past in the first days of June, meaning, "Take up your sickle in June!". In Poggioreale, as in other towns with a purely agricultural economy, there was an influx of seasonal immigration at the start of this month.

They were internal migratory flows which moved from the cities of the neighboring areas to the countryside, where the demand for labor was more pressing at the beginning of the harvest.

So already from the first days of the month, many daily workers moved to the country waiting to be hired.

Poorly dressed, with a shoulder bag, a blanket, and some modest provisions, they found shelter in the open space in front of the Church delle Anime Sante (Armisanti) located in Piazza Elìmo in front of Corso Umberto I.

Bored and tired during the day, you saw them sitting on the sidewalks or seeking the shelter of some tiny shadow that the houses projected at the corners of the streets; at night they stretched out their blankets and laid down next to each other, like many soldiers camped out in the open. If in the late evening some of the "borgesi" approached, many stood up in silence, expressing their exasperated anxiety to be chosen with their eyes alone.

The most depressing and mortifying scene of all was the choice of the number of workers needed. The employer, as if he were reviewing military fighters, carefully examined each worker from head to toe, eliminating the older ones, those who seemed physically fragile, choosing the younger ones, the more robust and those whose physical presence appeared of indubitable strength.

These were humiliating scenes that severely offended a man's personal dignity and left traces of indignation in anyone who had a minimal amount of sensitivity and awareness of human rights.

The implorations of the workers who realized they were being cast aside were translated into phrases like: "Hire me, please! Put me to the test, please! I'll be as good at the work as the others. Do it out of charity, for my children who have no bread at the table!"

Others instead walked away silently without uttering a word, their faces deeply marked by the mortification, resting their backs on the corner of a street, their eyes absent, their souls shaken. And many of those passed over, once the hirings had ended, returned home in a beaten-down state of abandonment of every initiative, hoping only for the help of providence.

4) *Other and profound evaluations must be expressed - together with the photos chosen and recovered In order to be reproduced In this book – for the unique images of the painting of Gianbecchina, faithful interpreter of the whole world of tools, works and customs, which now relive in the traits of the Maestro himself who has immortalized them with all the power of his participatory sensitivity. Having obtained permission to reproduce a selection of Gianbecchina's ethnological masterpieces was in fact another fortunate determination that adds to the inimitable quality of Vella's work, as well as the unique opportunity to find it accompanied and complemented by art of the most significant naive painter of Sicilian 20th century art.*

Lastly, the occasional preface author called to testify on the moral and scientific merits of this book cannot help but evaluate the context of the consent in favor of Erasmo Vella's historical work, which came from the cultural sensitivity of the pro-tempore Mayor of Poggioreale di Sicilia, engineer Pietro Vella, of his Council and of the entire Municipal Council, whose choice must be recognized for having provided the cities of today and of future generations with this precious document of history and civilization.

Mario Grasso, April 2003

Editor's Note:
Professor Mario Grasso is acknowledged in the original text, Page 199, as being the literary director for the publishing house, Prova d'Autore.

Chapter Titles

I	**Origins in the Historical and Social Context of the Time**
II	**Social Classes and Relations between Owners and Peasants**
III	**Colonial Pacts**
IV	**Protests and Revolts**
V	**Location of the Town**
VI	**Connections**
VII	**Land and Rural Roads**
VIII	**Education**
IX	**The Home**
X	**Home Furnishings**
XI	**The Family**
XII	**The Farmer's Work**
XIII	**Sowing**
XIV	**The Harvest**
XV	**"La Stravuliàta" and Threshing**
XVI	**Transporting the Wheat "La Carriata di lu Furmentu"**
XVII	**Folklore and Festivals**
XVIII	**Holy Christmas**
XIX	**New Year**
XX	**Carnival**

XXI	St. Joseph
XXII	The Festivity of St. Anthony of Padua
XXII	Folklore and Life Cycle
XXIV	Poggioreale from the Post-War Period to the 1968 Earthquake
XXV	From the Earthquake of January 14, 1968 to the Reconstruction of the New Town
XXVI	Reconstruction
XXVII	The New Poggioreale

Book Photos

The original text included 8 digital reproductions of paintings credited to the Italian artist known as Gianbecchina. Giovanni Becchina was born in Sicily in 1909 and died in 2001.

Also included in the text are 32 photographs from various sources. We have digitally reproduced them for your reference.

I - ORIGINS IN THE HISTORICAL AND SOCIAL CONTEXT OF THE TIME

It is impossible to trace the historical profile of a town without seeing it in the context of the region in which it originated, developed, and was subjected to the influences of customs, culture, tradition, and social and political organization: characteristics that distinguish one region from another.

Speaking of the Sicilians, Gesualdo Bufalino[1] sees the island in the plural. In fact, he says: "... Unlike the other islands, whose inhabitants are a compact group of people by race, habits, and customs, in Sicily everything is disparate, mixed, changing as in the most hybrid of the Continents. Certainly, for those who were born there, the joy of feeling like being the navel of the world lasts a short time, because soon the suffering takes over of not knowing how to untangle, between a thousand curves and interweaving of blood, the thread of one's own destiny."

Due to its geographical position in the middle of the Mediterranean, Sicily suffered the domination of peoples from the most disparate regions, who all brought different civilizations.

But if it is true that the first populations of the island, the Sicani and the Siculi, suffered the overlapping of different civilizations, it is also true that through the excavations, the testimonies of the classical and ancient authors, it has been discovered that the aforementioned populations had a religion and a mythology, in which the seeds of numerous Sicilian superstitions of today are found.

This suggests that, even in the succession of different civilizations, the Sicilians have maintained character traits that have represented a constant over time.

If we wanted to identify these characteristics, we can say very roughly that the Sicilian has a profound expression, sound, but is not talkative. Pride, arrogance, jealousy, impetus for love and hatred, perseverance of fidelity and revenge, loyalty and generosity, respect for religion without renouncing superstitions: these are its main connotations among the thousand curves mentioned by G. Bufalino.

These traits characterized (and are still present in the elderly generations),

---

[1].Gesualdo Bufalino, *Cento Sicilie: Testimonianze di un ritratto* [100 Sicilies, Testimonials of a portrait], Nuova Italia editrice, Florence, 1993.

in the personality of the citizens of the Municipality of Poggioreale, founded at the end of the first half of the seventeenth century.

In the 17th century, Spain had control of the Italian situation. In fact, it dominated the whole of southern Italy with the reign of the two Sicilies and the North with the state of Milan.

Sicily was then the region of the barons, the poorly cultivated large estates (called *latifundia*) and the very poor peasants. The bourgeois classes were not consistent enough to prevent the intensification of the feudal system, revitalized as a resource for defense from the crises of the time, from the land owners who lived as recipients of income far from the fiefdom, numbed by idleness and effeminacy.

The relationship between the Spanish monarchy and the noble and baronial class was of mutual interest: on the one hand, the government needed the ruling class to guarantee its domination in the Kingdom of Sicily against the possible onset of claims by the city population with the support of the rural plebs, subject to the mortification of the most elementary human rights.

The barons showed indifference to political perspectives focusing on the island's independence from foreign domination, thus bartering the independence of Sicily with the privileges that the viceroys never ceased to accord. In fact, Count Olivares's warning to the viceroys, "You are everything with the barons, without them you are nothing" supports their superior affirmations.

The barons were small kings; within his own fiefdom, each administered justice and imposed tributes on the peasants who worked in their fiefdom. Their presence in Parliament was only a matter of prestige and they were not at all involved in parliamentary activities, as they had no interest in politics. They were interested in exploiting the farmers to whom they entrusted the concessions of land, imposing taxes and demanding free work from their concessionaires or confiscating animals and crops.

The government sometimes issued measures in defense of poor farmers in order to avoid excessive abuse, but it was only smoke and mirrors, because these measures were never actually implemented. In fact, only the rich could send the king their petitions for the reparations of a wrong. As mentioned before, they appointed judges, owned underground prisons, and could torture prisoners or sentence them to death. The inquisitor had the right of appeal to the Court, but this constituted an offense to the baron and the applicant was then persecuted every which way until he was forced to abandon everything and flee to another place. Thus the rich, having attained the rank of nobility, bought jurisdiction for their territories at a high price.

The aristocrats therefore leaned on this parasitic exploitation of the poor and never acted to invest their income in activities that could improve the economy of the island. In fact, they considered trading shameful, considering it degrading work for example; and not only that, they also showed disinterest in agriculture, rejecting any active economic role. Thus they were absentee owners, attracted by the splendor of the Court and the comforts of city life. They were so extravagant as to mortgage their properties and cede their management to the new class of *gabellotti* (rural entrepreneurs often associated with the mafia).

The income of the land was unproductively exploited in the sense that it was used to increase a family's position through the acquisition of privileges compared to other noble families of the same rank, or to buy the prestige of keeping their heads covered before the viceroy or calling themselves "First class Grandees of Spain."

As the rich became barons, the families of ancient nobility sought to distinguish themselves from the new families by buying positions of superiority.

The first Marquises, a new title, were created in the 14th century according to some data provided by Mack Smith[2].

In the 16th century there were already seven newly inaugurated Counts, and in the 17th century this number reached 21. The first title of prince was bought by the head of the Butera family in 1563. Between 1620 and 1630, seven new duchies were created, 17 marquisates and 27 principalities.

Rivalry arose among the nobles who were classified above the new arrivals. This superiority had to be demonstrated with very expensive clothes, leading to the paradox of certain forms of gallantry such as keeping a greater number of servants than the others, displaying very expensive ceremonies. All this often achieved by borrowing money at high interest rates. In short, the rivalries between families sometimes had futile underlying motives, even including absurd claims for respect in establishing who should lead a procession or which among two carriages at an intersection in the narrow streets of Palermo should give way.

For Spain, the financial situation of the first half of the 1500s was negative and the second half was even worse: a period of economic crisis, social regression, and political decline. To face the Turkish expansionism that threatened the Spanish possessions, in 1571 King Philip joined the Holy League and fought against the Turks who were defeated in the battle of Lepanto, where the great clash between the Turkish and Christian fleets occurred. The expenses Spain incurred to deal with the conflict put the crown's

---

2. Mack Smith, A History of Sicily: Medieval Sicily 800-1713, Ed. Laterza, Bari.

Finances in serious crisis. In order to remedy it, the King severely increased taxes on his possesions.

The reflections the fiscal surge had on Sicily generated discord among the aristocracy that could not bear this burden.

But the economic crisis had fatal repercussions on the strata of the poor population, condemned to poverty and hunger.

The shift of commercial traffic following geographic discoveries, from the Mediterranean area to the Atlantic countries and the phenomenon of re-feudalization caused economic stagnation and a decline in agricultural production, with famines and epidemics becoming more frequent.

The legacy of the Middle Ages, which in the rest of Italy was in clear decline or had completely disappeared, would remain present in Sicily for a long time, following a rediscovered cohesion between the Spanish barony and monarchy.

In fact, in 1621 King Philip IV ascended the throne of Spain, who continued the policy introduced by his predecessor Philip III of Austria, 1598-1621. To calm the troubled waters throughout the Kingdom of Sicily, the king granted the baronial class other privileges. Moreover, having failed to carry out a large-scale project to reduce court expenses and impose legislation against luxury and waste on the nobles, given that due to economic instability and social torpor the State was unable to bear the costs of any military policy, the sales of titles and the planned colonization continued.

Thus the sovereign generously sold noble titles, which among other things benefitted from tax exemption. In addition, in order to keep the land-owning bourgeois and rural populations calm, internal colonization continued with more intensity, encouraged by the favorable economic situation of wheat trade. In fact, Garufi[3] argues wheat reached the price of 4.11[4] *oncie* for hard wheat and 3.24 *oncie* for soft wheat. The king and the nobles, especially those who had recently been appointed, had a mutual interest in remediating uncultivated and abandoned crops in order to increase the volume of grain crops. This program was also a focus of the Spanish government to improve the living conditions of farmers, who were encouraged to move to the newly established municipality with the promise of less onerous censuses and duties. This was a useful policy for temporarily halting the flaws of the moment, but it did not guarantee anything for the future.

The barons thus founded many municipalities, requesting "Licentia populandi" from the king. Many municipalities were founded in the most

---

3. C.A. Garufi, *Patti agrari e comuni feudali di nuova fondazione in Sicilia* [Agrarian pacts and newly established feuds in Sicily].
4. Oncie = metal coin equal to 15 lira or weight equal to 30 grams.

deserted and squalid areas of the large estates. To populate a feud, in addition to the "licentia populandi" request, the feudal lord had to pay a

variable sum to the tax authorities that could reach up to 200 *scudos*[5]. These expenses were added to those for the construction of the new habitable town.

From 1583 to 1653, more than 80 municipalities were founded. Among them, the Municipality of Poggioreale was founded in 1642 in the area of Bagnitelli following the concession obtained by the Marquis of Gibellina, Francesco Marchisio Morso. A heraldic genealogy of the Morso-Naselli family reads: "In execution of the aforesaid privilege, he ordered the construction of the Nelli Bagnitelli dwellings, a feud of the middle herd to populate the new land located below a hill on a wide plain, naming it Poggioreale, a delightful land of spacious plains variously adorned with hills and valleys."

In fact, as can be understood from the testimonies left by C. A. Garufi in the work already mentioned, the feudal lord first built the Church, then the warehouses, the mills, the taverns, the ovens, the slaughterhouses, and the streets. Then they moved on to the construction of houses for the new inhabitants. Generally, the testimonies show that few families declared ownership of their home; it was the feudal lord who built the houses and leased them to the settlers.

In order to encourage and incentivize work in the lands of the new dwellings, already in 1636 the Viceroy Duke of Montalto had urged the kingdom to help the peasants and the bourgeois with the aid of money and seeds. A certain exodus from the cities and neighboring towns to the newly established municipalities ensued. For the Municipality of Poggioreale, the initial population of 209 inhabitants consisted of the workers of the lands of the Bagnitelli feud and other families from Gibellina and even from the city of Mazara, which recorded a certain demographic decrease during the time.

The influx of settler families into the new feudal village was influenced by leasing concessions and the long leases for small extensions of land to farmers.

In fact, within a few decades of its foundation, the town experienced a significant increase in its population. It is impossible to trace a history of the town's developments from its foundation to the unity of Italy and beyond, because we have no sources from which to draw specific and distinctive social, cultural, economic and political information compared to other agricultural villages in the same district.

5. Scudo = metal coin equal to 2 lira.

Aside from a few transformations in the field of certain methods of working the land, while bearing in mind certain social and economic developments, the feudal mentality in relations, in the standard of living contained within the limits of survival remained largely unchanged until the end of World War Two.

The stages of evolution of the small agricultural villages were therefore so slow and delayed over such long periods that it is difficult to identify their consistency. Consider also that the Municipality of Poggioreale did not have civil and religious independence for about a century, meaning that full autonomy capable of favoring differentiated historical paths compared to the neighboring municipalities of Salaparuta and Gibellina.

The progress of agriculture required radical transformations in the components of the rural world anchored in a solid peasant civilization, in a world of ethical and cultural values that was very difficult to erase. The structuring of agricultural work revealed shortcomings due to the inability to integrate agricultural activities with livestock management. Intensive crops for forage were lacking; breeding needed large spaces and occupied vast expanses of uncultivated land. The soil's fertility was not restored through adequate fertilization, nor with frequent ploughing. Pastoralism was carried out in primitive forms based on the parasitic system of the simplest natural resources. Towards the end of the 1600s, the agronomic literature indicated more advanced farming techniques: the adoption of continuous rotations between grains and forage legumes, rotations that led to the abolition of periodic fallow land and grazing on uncultivated land. But the feudal system kept the people of the island away from these forms of innovation. While the most advanced land cultivation systems were exploited In the large farms of the North that were based on wage labor and oriented to the broader trading of their products, in our rural villages, on the other hand, the spirit of profit was seen as alien to the economy of survival and self-consumption. The sovereigns of Spain and the nobility were responsible for this "secular lethargy," who in order to preserve the immunities and privileges accorded by the viceroys, accepted the domination of the foreigner.

II. - SOCIAL CLASSES AND RELATIONS BETWEEN OWNERS AND PEASANTS

From what has been revealed (see the cited work of A.C. Garufi), it is clear that the population of the small island towns with a strictly agricultural economy had been stratified into several social classes since the 17th century. There were not only aristocrats on one side, represented by people of trust in the feuds, and working class and peasant people on the other, as in the past.

A land-owning *borghesia* had formed consisting of administrators, *gabelloti* and those above them who had exploited the absenteeism of the noble masters and their debts and had become rich.

The new landowners were favored by a law passed by Parliament during the revolts of 1647-48 which, subject to the approval of the viceroys, allowed the *borghesia* to acquire the property of the fallen nobles.

In the long and gradual process of decay of the feudal system, these "gentlemen" constricted the aspirations of the least disadvantaged peasants for the purchase of small lots of land, whose autonomous management could have relieved them of the state of submission in which they were forced to live.

The agrarian *borghesia* had consolidated itself as a phenomenon of gentrification even before the abolition of feudality with the government's provision of 1812. When ecclesiastical goods and pious works were sold, the poorest rural classes were almost completely excluded from the public auctions, even though they were tenants.

And so the massive intervention of the gentlemen at the public auctions led to the failure of the prospect of fractionation that the Church and the Pious Works had initiated with the concessions granted to the farmers. Next to the landowner *borghesia* were the middle and small owners who, through their tenacity at work and the use of certain intensive crops such as vineyards, had managed to become independent of the subjugation exercised by the owners of the feuds. Lastly there was also a *borghesia* consisting of traders and professionals, but very few in number. The lower level consisted of the rural plebs, those poor hungry people considered, in complete disregard of their miserable condition, as *plebaglia*, rabble.

This is the precise structure which also identifies the stratification in social castes of the Poggiorealese population.

However, the small and medium-sized landowners were not yet very widespread in the Municipality of Poggioreale; in the first decades of the 19th century 1,820 hectares of the territory, equal to 80% of its agricultural area, consisted of large estates, while the small peasant property totaled 14% of the entire area. This group of small Poggiorealese landowners expanded in the early 1900s following the economic resources coming, for many families, from the emigrants of America, whose flow had assumed significant proportions from the end of the 19th century until a few years after the First World War. With the division of the former feud of Cautalì in 1927, the number of landowners was increased.

In this regard, it should be recalled that the Archpriest Most Canonical Reverend Nunzio Caronna wrote a booklet entitled *L'Arch. Caronna al suo popolo* (Archpriest Caronna to his people) The book reports the speech he made to the people of Poggioreale in Piazza Elimo; an eloquent, effective, and vibrant speech full of expressions that grasp the harsh and miserable reality and condition of the farmers with deep emotion, inviting them to reflect, urging them to fight with determination until obtaining the division of the Cautalì feud from the "gentlemen" who administered the assets of the Congregation. This speech was given in 1914, but the division took place 13 years later, in 1927.

The legality of the feudal system was abolished in 1812, and finally completed with the two laws of August 2nd and 3rd in 1818. But the abolition of the nobles' legal power was transformed into de facto arrogance. The same *borghesia* took pleasure in imitating the nobles "following their absurd forms of vanity and arrogant attitudes." The gentleman considered the " *borgese* " and the "day laborer" as a means of gain or as land to be exploited.

With regard to the outrage with which the civilians treated the settlers, I find an episode that S. Costanza reports in the book *I giorni di Gibellina* (The days of Gibellina), on page 36[2] rather emblematic.

The Gibellinian peasants had asked for and obtained from their master, the Count of Comiso, the register of rents. Don Leonardo Lo Presti, administrator for the Morso Naselli family, opposed and provoked the *burgesi* by calling the honor of their women into question. The people became angry and hurled themselves against Lo Presti, who barely escaped, taking refuge in Salaparuta with the help of Arch. Calamia.

The agrarian *borghesia* that had become the landowner, which had previously been part of the feud, had therefore replaced the feudal lord in the depletion of resources through oppression

---

[1]Can. Dr. N. Caronna, *L'Arciprete Caronna al suo popolo* (Archpriest Caronna to his people), ed. Giuseppe Gianfala, Palermo 1914.
[2] Salvatore Costanza, *I giorni di Ghibellina,* ed. Flaccovio, Palermo.

At the beginning of the 19th century, the Intendant Baron of S. Gioacchino (another document cited by S. Costanzo) described the poverty of the laborers of Gibellina and the neighboring municipalities of Poggioreale and Salaparuta: "The large class of workers who are employed in the cultivation of the countryside, such hardships, such sweat costs them far more than their wages, which cannot suffice to maintain them that same day, what exhaustion of strength, what total fatigue does not afflict them. In those tasks requiring the robustness of man or the combined strength of animals, they cannot demand from the afflicted farmer but mechanical movements. What miserable condition of the productive class from which a portion of sweat is extorted in order to caress the softness of the rich and the idle." -19-

III - COLONIAL PACTS

The most common contracts between the *burgisi* and the owners were for rent or *gabelle*, sharecropping or "*colonia parziaria*" (individual plot of land), "*colonia a terratico*" (the rent of plots of land) and lastly that of "companion and master". There were other forms of contracts which, however, did not fall within the framework of the traditional bargaining dictated by the influence that the historical circumstances had on them.

The rent in Poggioreale generally lasted six years, but there were also four-year contracts.

The contract was stipulated per plots of land, i.e., every year upon the harvest, each *gabelloto* had to deliver to the owner the harvest from one, two or three plots of land according to the established agreements. If the agreement was for one plot of land, the tenant had to deliver one *salma*[1] of wheat for each *salma di terra*[2], or plot of land assigned in rent, if it was for two plots of land, then the tenant had to deliver two for each *salma di terra* and so on. Evidently, the agreements for one or two plots of land always depended on the nature of the land and its fertility; sharecropping lasted one year, that is, after the agrarian year had passed, the owner could dismiss the settler or reconfirm his use for as much time as was mutually agreed by both parties.

Generally, the following conditions were respected:

1) the owner assumed the burden of sowing the seed, upon harvest he expected double seed on the land fertilized by Hedysarum, or *sùlla* in Silician or by fava beans; so if two *salmas* of seed had been used for sowing, he took four *salmas* before dividing the harvest in half. Instead, the master took half the seed for the land cultivated the second time with wheat without the forage fertilization *(supra ristuccia)*, meaning that if he anticipated two *salmas* of wheat, he recovered them from the harvest before dividing it in half.

2) the rent of plots of land (*colonia a terratico*) generally followed the same conditions as the *gabelle*, except that the duration of the contract was always one year.

3) the contract for companion and master envisaged the division of the harvest to the extent of 2/3 for the owner and 1/3 for the companion. Clearly these

---

1 Salma = unit of measurement of grains equal to 220 kg of wheat.
2 Salma di terra = 3 and 20 hectares of land, according to local measurements.

contracts changed according to the claims of the owners and the state of necessity of the sharecropper who sometimes, due to lack of availability of work, had to suffer severe oppression, resigning himself to accepting harsh conditions: "*Càlati immo chi passa la china*" ("In some situations, it's best to pretend nothing has happened").

On average, the yield of each hectare of land, excluding the years of particularly scarce production due to certain weather events that left the sharecroppers or tenants without enough to feed the whole family, was about 110 lire, if cultivated with wheat, 175 if cultivated with sumac and 35 lire if cultivated with fava beans. These amounts in lire are very approximate, because the *gabelle* or rent was paid in nature and the yield in nature was translated into lire to give a more concrete idea of the yield that the farmer obtained with the immense efforts he put into the land.

In the larger feuds, the *borgese* had to use the revenues of the crops to cover the quota set for the feudal lord, that for the *gabellato* and in certain cases for the *sub-gabelloto*. For example, in a feud such as Cautalì Grande, the *gabellato* agreed on the amount owed to the feudal lord; in turn he sub-rented the land to another person with whom a contract was agreed that allowed him to cover the amount owed to the feudal lord and that for himself. The *sub-gabellato* in turn granted the part of the feud rented to different sharecroppers in lots, depending on the hectarage that each could take on in consideration of the equipment and workers they had available, provided by family members or by agreements made with other farmers. Within this hierarchical scale, regardless of the conditions agreed for supporting the production expenses, the poor farmer shouldered the onerous task of struggling day after day, between all kinds of hardships, difficulties, and tribulations in order to cover the agreed quotas and bring a small piece of bread home.

In addition, depending on the size of the company, the *borgese* had to add day wage earners *(iurnateri)*, monthly wage earners or annual wage earners. The day wage earners were paid 85 cents a day plus food or two lire a day without food up to the early 1900s. The annual wage earners received 155 lire a year with supplies or 450 lire without supplies, but usually the annual earners were forced to live on the farm in winter and summer with the possibility of enjoying the *vicenna*[3] once a month and were hired with the benefit of supplies.

Thus the tenant farmer or *metateri* was weighed down by so many duties

---

3. *Vicenna* = from the words vicenda-avvicendamento, it gave annual employees the opportunity to enjoy a few Sundays of rest with their families, for changing the linen.

and fees that thinned their profits. And although the price of grains rose somewhat after 1860, this did not bring any change, because the extension of the cultivated land remained unchanged until the 1930s, nor did the customs of rent and sharecropping change much until that date.

The municipal administrations were run by the gentlemen. The power to govern the Municipality was above all a prestige that could not be given to the illiterate farmer; but for some, it was also the way to exploit the office being held. And in the latter case the criterion for the division of the expenses that the Municipality faced was to privilege the interests of the ruling class, sometimes quite discretionary, rather than making life easier for the farmers with the construction of roads and a connection between the town and the countryside.

Simply to cite an example, as early as 1863 in Poggioreale, that is, immediately after the unification of Italy, many resolutions were issued for the construction of the municipal theater, which was only built and delivered ten years later in 1873. So rather than see to more urgent works, it was preferred to follow a trend that was quite widespread at the time very, that is, the desire to build theaters. For Poggioreale it was undoubtedly a work of public interest where people would have found at least some distraction from their ailments, but to tell the truth I do not believe that those who struggle to survive find serenity and the possibility of going to the theater.

The pious works were also administered by the ruling class and represented a source of easy profits for the less honest, while they were a motive of prestige, influence, and favoritism for the more honest. The "civil" abused their strength to satisfy the whim of keeping the people submissive and demand their respect in a unilateral sense: "I am the master and you who are in my service, you are my employee and as such I hold you in consideration." These were the customs of medieval life that were still present when Italy was unified, and continued afterwards for more than three quarters of a century, legalized by the Italian government.

IV - PROTESTS AND REVOLTS

The peasants and craftsmen were so accustomed to accepting their state that they passed it on to several following generations as a fate shaped by destiny, for which nothing could be hoped but to submit to God's will.

Not even the spread of the ideas of the Enlightenment that led to the French Revolution found any possibility of penetrating in Sicily. The efforts of the intellectuals aimed at reaching social structures inspired by the redemption of the island people from a state of subjugation and deprivation failed due to the obstacles dictated by the fear of novelty, by the consolidated habits in the people of the countryside to maintain their devotion and subjection to the feudal lord. In fact, when men like F. P. De Blasi, Francesco Rossi, Giuseppe Ardizzone fought to push the Sicilians to revolt, they did not have the support of the peasant masses.

It is true that the Bourbon government's underestimation of the peasants' state of misery had generated, under the urging of liberal groups, some turmoil of intolerability, but it is also true that the tolerance with one's own state limited any momentum. However, the reflections of the movements of 1820, 1848, 1860 also reached the Belice Valley, and the rural villages of Poggioreale, Salaparuta and Gibellina were home to some uprisings of the poor which, exploiting the circumstance and driven by exasperation and despair, degenerated into forms of uncontrolled protest aimed at redemption from a bitter condition of slavery, servility and misery. On some occasions, the forces and fury of the population were unleashed in manifestations of violence, which in the delirium of hunger uncorked hatred and resentment against those who were pleased to keep them submissive and bound to a life of hardship and suffering. The crowd that went down to the square to protest was considered a mob that had nothing to lose: no goods, no restraint, no values, nor character. Thus the revolts were not even supported by certain parts of the peasant population who, although occupying one small step of the social ladder above the others and suffering the same abuses, did not dare to meddle among the crowd of so-called *scalmanati* (hotheads).

And it was for this resigned acceptance of one's own condition of life and for the strict principles of restraint, extending so far as to protect the submission to those of respect, that many revolts failed and ended with the gallows and arrests, especially in the large inhabited towns.

The movements of 1848 were felt in Poggioreale, arousing the protest above all of the working class. But the entire subordinate population certainly did not participate. Don Giuseppe Campisi was responsible for public order at the time, as the first elected in the municipal administration who, thanks to the collaboration of Archpriest Don Vincenzo Agosta, a man who imposed himself for his prestige, easily managed to quell the protest, preventing the Bourbons from having to resort to the use of the gallows or prison. And in 1860 it was again Don Giuseppe Campisi to control the antagonistic ferments between the Bourbons and Italians, avoiding the unleashing of the popular classes' rage. When demonstrations of the working classes degenerated into bloody events in the nearby city of Gibellina in 1893, the president of the working classes of Poggioreale, Don Ignazio Asaro, was able to curb the crowd's unrest. In fact, the security measures of curfew and the delivery of weapons were applied in Poggioreale, but no one was ever convicted (see the story of Can. Aloisio)[1].

As previously stated, this composure reflects the attitude of tolerance in respecting the gentlemen, with whom the peasants, the "*borgesi*", the small landowners, wanted to maintain relationships of dependence centered on the sense of serene acceptance and disguised by an external appearance of mutual friendship.

The people of Poggioreale were much more tumultuous in 1920, when the poor peasants occupied the uncultivated lands of the large estates in the South. There was consistent uproar in the crowd of peasants surrounding the office of the Congregation in order to obtain the possession of those lands. The famous ride of the Poggiorealese peasants for the occupation of the former Pietra feud also deserves mention. As in the other inhabited towns, these manifestations of the struggle did not devolve into merciless episodes of blood between the owners and peasants.

In this regard, Can. F. Aloisio affirms that the people, deceived by the speeches of the socialists who encouraged them to charge, instilling the vision of riches being quite near, had shamelessly lost control, giving rise to a tumultuous period with the occupation of lands of the former Pietra feud.

Undoubtedly the speeches of the socialists had incited the crowd to protest, to occupy the uncultivated lands of the feuds, emphasizing the very reasons for the dispute, with the result of generating confusion and anger in the minds of the people, the successors of centuries-long submission.

---

[1]Can. Francesco Aloisio, *Storia di Poggioreale* (History of Poggioreale), Tipolitografia Priulla, Palermo, 1986; reprint.

In truth, the speeches inciting the masses of peasants were founded in the promises that the government had made and not kept at the end of the First World War.

We know that in 1915 the interventionists, members of the Italian *borghesia*, decided to participate in the war against the opposition of the workers, who then represented the largest part of the army in war. In order to obtain the unconditional participation of these social forces in the war, as well as to resort to coercive means, they promised the land to the peasants: "After the victorious end, Italy will carry out a great act of social justice... this is the reward offered by the homeland to its valiant children." At the end of the war, not one of the promises made was kept. This provoked a great deal of discontent that drove the crowds mad.

It should also be recalled that agricultural cooperatives had been created in many areas of the various Italian regions. Through the Visocchi Decree, these cooperatives had obtained the concession from the Italian government to occupy the uncultivated estates of the large landowners for a certain number of years depending on the type of cultivation. If then the speeches aimed at urging the people to protest to wake up from a certain numbness and demand improvements in their social status led to effects that caused the protesting crowd to lose control, this does not justify the reference to the phrase of A. Schopenhauer: "The common people resemble dogs, who love to be caressed and thrown bones."

Those who encouraged the people towards the social and economic redemption for a free and democratic life could not identify with those who exploited and leveraged the condition of the poor for personal gain, and if there was an instrumental pretext, all the better if this came to benefit the subordinate classes. And if the protests in Poggioreale only brought minor improvements to some contractual relations, the same cannot be said for other agricultural towns, where the associations obtained new rights against the owners' privileges. In fact, the small tenants, the shareholders obtained mandates that the collective agreements were obligatory. With these contracts, it was no longer the farmer negotiating conditions with the owner, but the workers' organizations in cooperatives.

The contracts were previously based on the custom of "*terzeria*", a system under which the owners took two thirds of the product without incurring any expenses, leaving the farmer with a third part. As in all sharecropping contracts, the seeds, fertilizers, and other products used in agriculture were the responsibility of the sharecroppers.

With the new contracts, however, the owners were obliged to bear half of the expenses for the seeds and natural and chemical fertilizers. It is however true that these conquests lasted very little time, because the large agricultural companies began to prepare their counter-offensive to regain the lost privileges. In fact, in 1920 fascism turned out to be a terrorist organization of the land and industrial *borghesia*, disguised as propaganda that encouraged the peasants to follow the fascist movements, because fascism presented itself as a "friend of the peasants," and would save the small landowners, lifting up the peasant economy. But in the meantime, Decree No. 2023 of December 10, 1923 declared the occupation of uncultivated land illegal, which had previously been legalized by the provincial commissions. Thus all the poor peasants and war veterans were driven from the lands that they then saw returned to the owners fertile, plowed and rendered productive with their sweat and tenacious hard work.

The same law abolished the prohibition imposed on landowners from increasing the rent demanded of small tenants and the other prohibition on removing tenants from land under concession at the end of the contract, unless there were serious reasons to justify the measure.

The reaction to the legislative provision of 1923 was stifled by the regime's extensive propaganda on the two most important agrarian policy initiatives of fascism: "The Battle of Wheat" and the "Integral Reclamation." Propaganda that Giuseppe Di Vittorio then denies in a booklet published in Paris in 1929.

In fact, when visiting Sicily again in 1937, Mussolini announced to the Sicilians that an era was approaching for our island that had never before occurred in its 4,000 years of history and promised the liquidation of the large estates and extensive agriculture. His words had no credibility, as the people, disappointed with the same promises made in 1923, believed that it would again simply be propaganda to fill the newspapers. But in fact, his political position was beginning to take on a new face, the anti-bourgeois one. However, when he decided to implement this program, it was too late because only a few years later the war broke out.

V - LOCATION OF THE TOWN

Poggioreale is built on the slopes of Mount Elimo or Mount "Le Rose," today commonly called *Castellaccio*. Before the earthquake of January 14, 1968, the town had a medieval structure which was well suited to the needs of the agricultural population of the time. The mother church, the staircase that connects with the square and the main street were the town's central nodes, around which the homes developed among a network of well-cut roads which, within the overall framework, reconciled design needs with the need to adapt to the nature of the land chosen for the location of the town. I believe the reference point from which the entire town developed was the palace of Marquis Don Francesco Marchisio Morso, which was his summer residence.

The town was built 400 meters above sea level on a hilly terrain with a more accentuated slope in the north area of the main road and more moderate heading south.

The particular geological nature of the land, which was considered substantial, determined the town's location. It is true that there have been telluric movements and landslides (including the large crack in the northwest of the town that occurred about a century ago, the collapse of Monte Castellaccio in the northeast in 1890 and lastly the tectonic movement of 1954, which created deep crevices over 300 hectares of land, without however damaging any of the town's buildings), but it is also true that the earthquake of 1968 caused the roofs of the houses to collapse while the perimeter walls of the houses remained standing, a testament to the consistency of the land.

In fact even today, 30 years after the earthquake, the ghost town (to those who look at it from a distance) still seems intact, indicating to future generations the memory of the past of our fathers, of our grandfathers, who stood there in those streets, lived in those houses in suffering and joy, in pain and resignation, in simplicity and in the love for their family.

According to some data provided by the historian Salvatore Costanza[1], the population of 209 inhabitants in the first decade of the town's foundation then significantly increased. In fact, in just over half a century, in 1714 there were

---

[1] Salvatore Costanza, *I giorni di Ghibellina* (The Days of Ghibellina), Ed. Flacovio, Palermo.

1,097 inhabitants. This increase continued in the following years: in 1748 there were 1,822 and in 1798 it reached 3,000 inhabitants.

In the following century the demographic increase experienced periods of stagnation due to some migratory movements towards America, towards other municipalities of Agrigento, due to certain flows of temporary or permanent displacement in the neighboring lands of Monreale.

In fact, in the book *Vita civile di Poggioreale*[1] by Archpriest Nunzio Caronna, a man of deep culture and versatile writer, it states that more than 1,000 individuals from Poggioreale had been scattered here and there in various regions of America since the early years of the 20th century, causing the suffering of families, disrupting family affections and separating relatives.

After the Great War (1915-18), there was a large increase in emigration to the Americas; the migratory flow was only partly compensated by the immigration of the poor coming from Alcamo and Gibellina itself, attracted by the help that was offered by the acts of welfare extended at the time. The phenomenon of demographic decline paused in certain phases thanks to the intervention of fascism, which aimed at increasing the population by providing certificates of merit to large families.

We already know from highly accredited sources (Aloisio quoted above and the *Memorie Storiche* of Arch. Nunzio Caronna)[2], that for its ecclesial office, Poggioreale has always belonged to the Diocese of Mazara and was part of the territorial and political jurisdiction of Gibellina, when the latter became the capital of the *mandamento* (district). The town's inclusion in the province of Trapani occurred following the royal decree with which Sicily was divided into seven provinces in 1821. The transition from Palermo to Trapani caused great discontent in the population and the Municipality made many attempts to be reintegrated in the province of Palermo, but its attempts were all useless despite the plausible reasons considering its proximity compared to Trapani, the more frequent relationships the town's inhabitants had with Palermo and for the familiarity that trade relations had created between the town and the city.

---

[1] Can. Arch. N. Caronna, *Vita civile di Poggioreale* (Civil Life of Poggioreale), Tipografia Pontificia, Palermo 1906.
[2] Can. Dr. N. Caronna, *Memorie storiche di Poggioreale,* (Historic Memories of Poggioreale) Palermo 1901.

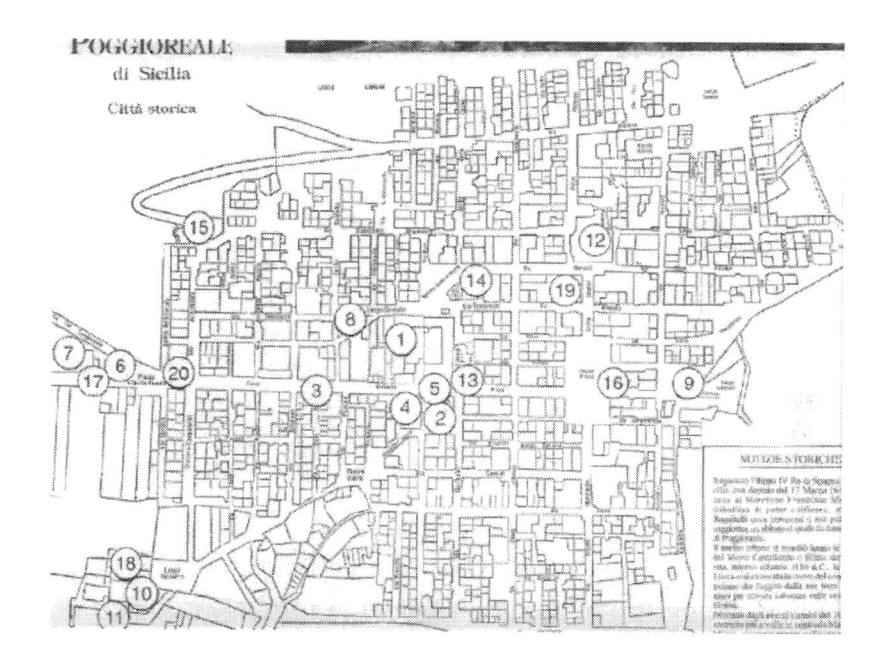

Photo 1 - Layout of the old town.
-29-

Photo 2 - Piazza and Mother Church, historic town
-30-

Photo 3 - Corso Umberto, historic town

VI - CONNECTIONS

The connections with the towns of the district, with the other larger towns of the province and with Palermo were not favored by adequate carriage roads. The General Lieutenant saw to the problem in 1844 and entrusted the drafting of the project to architect Don Gaspare Di Giovanna. For 20 years the initiative was then abandoned. The Provincial Council reconsidered the project in 1861, when many municipalities were already connected by carriage roads.

The project that included the completion of the roads connecting Poggioreale and Salaparuta with Gibellina, and Gibellina with S. Ninfa, Partanna, and Alcamo was approved in 1870 and completed ten years later, in 1880.

At that time a railway station was built in Gallitello on the Palermo-Castelvetrano railway line. This favored the connection with Palermo and the other large towns of the province, although its distance from Poggioreale was a significant inconvenience for those who needed to travel. A courier was set up connecting the three towns with the railway station for the transport of passengers and the mail. Poggioreale would have to wait until 1925 to take advantage of the railway station of Salaparuta.

The establishment of the telegraph service in 1873 and of a second-class post office ten years later facilitated communications, with a gradual reduction in the isolated state of families, even if travel was quite difficult for them at least until a few years after the Second World War; that is, until roads were established with convenient and efficient buses. In fact, the Poggiorealese did not have the comfort of a railway line in their own town and were forced to use that of Salaparuta about three kilometers away, whose connection was carried out with the mail courier. Passengers who needed to travel by train used this means when the train schedules were compatible with those of the postal service; otherwise, they had to reach the train station by foot, riding mules or with rental cars if they could afford it.

Around the 1930s, it began to be possible to reach Palermo or other cities in the province by using car rental services, guaranteed by the presence of local rental companies, as long as those renting the cars could pay for them. Thus the discomfort of our people who have never been able to have a train station in a peripheral area of the town was one more reason for its state of isolation compared to the neighboring towns.

In fact, if there was a need to travel by train at four o'clock in the morning, the traveler was forced to wander the streets by foot at night with the risk of being stripped of everything he carried: there were often bad encounters with robbers. To cite just one example, immediately after the fall of fascism and the armistice between Italy and the Americans, criminal organizations flourished, seriously straining the tranquility and safety of the Poggiorealese population due to the frequent thefts perpetrating the towns and cities. It was during this period that the road connecting with the train station of Salaparuta intimidated and frightened anyone who needed to take the train in the early morning hours or travel home from the station after dark. Thugs abounded almost every night, evading the vigilance of the carabinieri.

Mention must be made of an episode that falls somewhere between comedy, fear and indignation. The young Poggiorealese men received the notice to appear before the commission for army conscription in the city of Partanna. Having to show up in the early hours of the morning, the young men had to take the train at four a.m. Fearing unexpected delays, they set out at two o'clock in the morning. To prevent them all from being halted by any robberies, they sent a first group ahead that signaled their presence on the road by playing the guitar and mandolin. The others followed at a distance and as long as the musical notes brightened their way, they followed worry-free.

The first group was about a kilometer from Salaparuta when they received the threatening order: "Hands up! Everybody off the road and lie face down!" And meanwhile one of the robbers pointed a gun at the musicians, forcing them to continue playing and singing aloud, while the other two in the meantime stole watches, wallets, everything that the friends in the group were wearing. The boys' plan failed and all the groups that followed found themselves face down on the ground for long hours. In fact, they were not allowed to move until the first light, nor to ask for help from any passers-by: a rifle was pointed at them from behind the parapet of a wall. This was their strict order under the threat of death while the robbers, having no further travelers to steal from, walked away leaving those poor boys to breathe in the acrid odors of the wet earth without even being able to find solace in counting the stars.

VII - LAND AND RURAL ROADS

The land of Poggioreale has not undergone any variations and its surface area totals 3,608 hectares according to the data reported by Canon Aloisio in the aforementioned work and extends for the most part over hills, with the exception of the *dagali,* flat lands near the Belìce riverbed. The *dagali* of our land extend from the point of confluence along the right arm of the river, to the bridge and beyond and along the left arm to the Grotta Nera district and beyond, but always in relation to the entire strip along the eastern slope of the Cautalì Grande Mountain. Downwards from the confluence, the surface of the *dagali* widens due to the presence of more frequent recesses, due to the gentler slope of the river bed and the more consistent flow of the waters, when the Belice was a river. The connection between the town and the land was a road network consisting of *trazzere* (Sicilian peasant tracks), paths and mule tracks which were quite challenging, especially in the rainy season. Even if the main roads had been cobbled with pebbles or with solid rock obtained from the areas near the road itself, the wear of the long years and the lack of maintenance had regardless affected them, making it difficult to transit in some places even by the pack animals. In fact, until the 1940s, when the town's people saw a horse muddied up to its neck entering the special washhouse, or *lavaturi*, right next to the trough of the "cannoli" area, a common saying was that "this beast comes from under the Scala", a peasant track that was difficult to travel in the winter season.

The main arteries of the countryside roads of that time have not changed up to today, except for a few variations. These include: the carriage road that from the northern part of the town leads to the old cemetery; this branches into two arms, one connects the town with the districts of Madonna, Pioppo, Saccurafa, the northwestern slope of Mount Castellaccio, Spinapulce; the other branches into three other roads connecting with the districts of Giammaritaro, Giagati, and once with the former mill "del serpente" and, passing the river at the former pass (ford) of "l'agnuni" with the valley of Cautalì Grande and piccolo; a second road connected the district of Giagati up to the "Mulè" pass and from there to the valley of Cautalì Piccolo; a third descended towards the Carbone bridge to connect with the district of the same name and other nearby areas; on the northwest side the road to S. Antoninello, which leads to the districts Abita, Zotta di pernice, Macchia, Ovario and the archaeological area of Mount Castellaccio; on the southeast side the road to Marrasini which leads to the districts Montagna, Marrasini, Asparacia, Guardiola, and in the past the former mill above, and from the homonymous river pass to Cautalì Grande; another branch led to the former "*la prisa*" (water well for the operation of the mills) for the districts "tre pezzi" and "diano"; the carriage road to S. Margherita Belice, which leads to the districts Paradiso, Mandria di mezzo, Dagala della donna, Corridore, the former middle mill and other lands; on the south side of the town there are also the peasant tracks "li pili" and the other of "li vruchiceddi" which lead to the districts of the same name; on the east side the carriage road Poggiore-Salaraputa leads to the "orto" and "donna rosa" districts.

The road network of the countryside is now almost entirely drivable using mechanical vehicles and cars.

Our land borders the Belìce River to the south. Over the centuries this river has also been called lpsa or Crimìso, as well as "flumen magnum" for the flow of water it had in ancient times. If the Poggiorealese, at least as much as concerns their land, had had to give the river a name, they would have called it "our river," because in the overall picture of the things that were familiar to them, this watercourse has always occupied a prominent place for the continuous contact they had with it both to cross it in order to reach the work areas, and for the cultivation of the adjacent lands. The water of the river was precious, it was where cattle, herds of sheep, work animals and recreational animals quenched themselves; it was where housewives went to wash their clothes in the summer due to the lack of water, where they went to fish for eels, flathead mullet, crabs, tench and in more remote times trout and mullet, where they went hunting for migratory and permanent game. Among the migratory game, coots passed through starting in October, and teals, ducks, mallards and many other species of anatids were very precious; the grey heron and the woodcock both found a suitable environment in the various reeds that were then very common in all the *dagali*; the curlews, lapwings, and snipes were attracted by the prevalent marshes of the river basin. The permanent game that was hunted included moorhens, the rabbits that proliferated among the widespread scrub of many uncultivated areas and the foxes. In addition, the Poggiorealese frequently visited the river due to the need to cut the reeds and flexible buds of the elm tree to make large cane baskets for harvesting, bread baskets and those for daily use. Our farmers were experts at making these tools; indeed, some were real artists in building objects and miniature baskets that were real jewels. The townsfolk also visited the river due to the need to procure wood for the winter and to go grind wheat at the mills powered by water that existed in the area at the time, and were considered relaxing meeting places for the customers as they waited their turn.

The very gradual improvement of the road network allowed the peasant people who had been isolated within the walls of the agricultural village and within the boundaries of the work environment to perceptibly open up their mentality, less constrained by the mental closed-mindedness in which they were forced to live due to customs, to being used to it, by the will of the ruling class and in more remote times even by the clergy.

In fact, in the last years of the 19th century some extra-agricultural activities began, artisan activities spread further, there was a greater increase in the home textile industry; in fact, there were about 70 looms in Poggioreale in that time, a much higher number than in Salaparuta and Gibellina itself. Moreover, there was more widespread sensitivity towards public education, although this was very inconsistent considering the very high percentage of illiterates.

Photo 4 - Ancient Loom

VIII- EDUCATION

From a report drawn up by the school inspector Spallicci in 1870, it appears that there had already been a night school in Poggioreale (previously mentioned work by S. Costanza) before one was established in Gibellina and that the Municipality's interest in education was more sensitive than the other municipalities in the area. In fact, at that time Poggioreale spent about 62 cents per inhabitant, while Gibellina spent only 45 cents.

In those years there was initially a first and second-year elementary school class (see the previously mentioned work by Can. F. Aloisio), and subsequently thanks to the initiative of the priest Don Giuseppe Caronna, also a third and a fourth-year elementary school class. In the years that followed and until 1923, the elementary schools operated in a disjointed, non-continuous manner, at least in relation to the fourth and fifth-year classes and as regards the girls. The pardon from compulsory schooling was dictated by rural families' need to use their young children for light work and services. Their contribution to the work was essential for helping the whole family.

The high percentage of illiterates was also desired by the ruling class as well as by the clergy in much more remote times which, as a general guideline, did not encourage the education of the faithful.

The state of misery and ignorance, diseases and pestilence intensify religious fervor. Those who suffer implore divine Providence to intervene to relieve them of illness and need and resign themselves to the will of God. The priest was the most representative figure for comforting the sufferer, to whom he gave the hope of a future divine justice, to compensate him for the present one. The priest, therefore, is the one who gives the farmer not only the comfort of faith, but is the one who respects him as a man.

Responding to some queries from the Ministry to investigate the reasons behind such a high percentage of illiterates in the South and in Sicily in particular, the school inspector Cassone drafted a report that reads as follows: "The clergy can be divided into two orders, the astute and the simpletons; I will make no mention of the truly good, which although they exist, are few and far between. The simpletons oppose education through ignorance and most of the time are nothing but spokespersons. The clever ones pretend to believe that popular education is dangerous, that it is to the detriment of religion and they would prefer that the masses knew nothing but how to write."

Moreover, if the clergy did not encourage education, this was to prevent the masses from inculcating ideas aimed at overthrowing the existing social state with disturbances and violence that would always hurt the weakest the most.

A passage entitled *L'elogio dell'ignoranza¹* (The Praise of Ignorance) by Giuseppe Bonetta reads: "... to tear the children from their father's house to instruct them by force is an abuse of public power. Moreover, the school being able to be, both with regard to politicians and the religious, contrary to the ideas of the father of the family or of those who legitimately hold the place thereof, compulsory education is contrary to religious and civil freedom; therefore, children would be forced to imprint their minds in one way or another according to the ideas and influences of the state in public schools, influences that are not always considered beneficial... From this arises the presumption of knowledge in the plebs, the desire to interfere in public things that are poorly understood; from this arises the easy means of imprinting the most subversive doctrines, discontent, distrust against everyone and everything in their crude minds... which leads to the decay of moral sentiment, the clouding of the conscience of good and evil, the propensity to the savage war of the poor against the rich."

Therefore, the absence from school up to the 1920s led to a very high percentage of illiterates and semi-literates. According to the data reported by Can. F. Aloisio, the continuous operation of a fifth-year male class had to wait until 1922 thanks to the initiative, after approval by the Regional School Council, of the meritorious Maestro Aloisio. The establishment of a compulsory public school in an almost feudal reality was considered a strange and unacceptable imposition given the state of poverty of the peasants who struggled to survive.

Thus education was limited to the achievement of the simple objective of reading, writing and being able to do simple math.

Subsequently the elementary schools, although quite uncomfortable due to the inadequacy of the premises resulting from the adaptation of private houses used as school classrooms, functioned as regulators with a gradual decrease in the percentage of illiterates and semi-literates and with the promotion of a noticeable tendency of some families of the middle and craftsmen class to send some of their children to study, perhaps choosing for the younger children the religious schools of the Seminary of Mazara del Vallo, free of charge for youth

1. Giuseppe Bonetta, *Istruzione e società nella Sicilia dell'Ottocento*, (Education and Society in 19th-century Sicily), Sellerio editore, Palermo 1881.

who wanted to follow the path of the priesthood.

Since that time, the town had had a library that was a great privilege for the small agricultural town, a privilege which was then for the few readers who had curiosities and cultural interests, while today it is a rich source of culture for the consultation of its substantial library endowment.

The library has a particularly interesting heritage of books, which come from the Capuchin Fathers and whose editions range from 1500 to 1831. The Superintendency of Cultural Heritage of Trapani has taken care to inventory them by delegating expert staff for the purpose and with the collaboration of the librarian, Mrs. Maria Crocchialo in Milazzo, who has carried out the work for several years with interested participation and expertise.

The ancient books inventoried include: 730 editions from the 18th century, 75 from the 17th century, 14 from the 16th century, plus an ensemble in two volumes from 1853, in large format with a valuable binding, and 11 manuscripts from the 18th century.

The library has a total of 8,834 books. Poggiorealese readers have registered a significant increase in their interest in reading, especially in the last decade, considering that the movement of books loaned and consulted on site increased from 112 books in 1991 to around 1,000 in 2001.

For a town with an agricultural economy, it is an interesting prerogative to provide a rich source of consultation and reading, and it is an irreplaceable teaching aid especially for primary and secondary school children, so that they are educated to develop cultural information processes through frequent research provided by the educational projects developed and pursued by the teachers. Now that there is a broad, uncontrolled viewing of television programs, developing children's interest in reading is one of the priority objectives in the context of school activities, extended throughout the students' progression through their various stages of growth.

Photo 5 - School Group
-41-

IX- THE HOME

Fuculareddu miu! Casuzza mia - tu sì reggia e sì batia! (Hearth of mine! Little house of mine - you are a palace and a convent!) This expression embodies a deep feeling that evokes the soundness and intimacy of the family, whose balance had the home as its first cornerstone. Indeed, the home is the palace, the temple, the place of rest from daily fatigue.

The homes in Poggioreale responded to the needs, habits, and economic possibilities of the family. The architecture of the first houses very briefly followed ancient straw huts, gradually replaced by masonry. In fact, the first constructions of the new town were for the most part earthen houses made with stone and mud *(taju),* whose coverage was given by sloping roofs with channels. This led to the typical urban home consisting of four walls, a roof, and a door.

With the demographic increase, a certain evolution was achieved that allowed a more rational division of the environments. The ground floor was used for work, especially by craftsmen who used the floor for their workshop, but it was intended more broadly as a stable for sheltering animals, as a haystack for supplies of straw and hay and as a warehouse for firewood and various work tools.

The next floor was where the intimate life of the family was located: generally, for many families of the "*borgesato*", there were two rooms used as both bedrooms and a living room, with an adjacent kitchen.

Some houses instead had only one room above in which to sleep, while the kitchen and oven were carved out of the ground floor room used as a stable. This was certainly not a hygienically healthy and easy accommodation, but the family members found themselves there in the long winter evenings, serene and comforted by the warmth of the domestic hearth, by the warmth that was breathed and penetrated into the soul of each person, strengthening the bonds of affection and love.

The rooms above were usually accessed through an internal staircase that led through a hatch, *catarrattu*, into the compartment that covered it, or through an external staircase resting against the perimeter wall and supported by an arch that served as a porch and often as an entrance to the ground floor.

Some houses followed the principle of isolation that had already been adopted by the Aegean-Mycenaean homes, Greco-Roman homes, and the Arabs. Not very widespread in Poggioreale, these houses did not open towards the street except with small windows, while they received light and air from the courtyards around which they developed.

The kitchen was usually located in a small separate room; imitating the hearth in the stables of the other homes, it was composed of two masonry stoves, one of which was wider for the larger copper pots: the *quadara lu quadaruni*, or *quadaredda*[1], and the other narrower stove for the smaller pots of enameled terracotta for making sauces: tomato sauce, *sarsa*, stewed meat and other less bulky dishes. The wood to feed the fire was indispensable in every house and therefore very highly sought; like straw, with which the oven was heated for making bread, wood was equally necessary and abundant supplies were required to meet daily needs during the year.

The chimneys that rose from the roofs filled the air with smoke, especially at nightfall, and travelers arriving from the countryside cold and tired would look from the top of the hill or from the rocky heights of S. Francesco and feel a sense of well-being and solitude to see them. That smoke was the scent of wood, it was the scent of the modest dishes that the woman of the house prepared with love and dedication while waiting for the father of the family to come home; the sensation he got from this emphasized his thoughts, his imagination, so much so that he felt pride upon seeing the small village, because the fusion of the smoke that emanated from the various chimneys was interpreted as an expression of the communion of affections among the people and a symbol of the life that thrived throughout the town. Yes, it is true, his people were in those houses leaning against each other, his family, his friends, his relatives, his own world, his own life. Thus the beauty of the scene absorbed all his attention.

Today the chimneys are no longer visible and no longer indicate the fervor of the past life to travelers, but the silence, abandonment, sunset, night, the tomb-like peace of the cemeteries instead create feelings of fear, dismay, emotion and regret.

Yet the farmer, now elderly, who observes the panorama from one of the many hills, his village, the old and dear village where he was born and lived and where he left the hard years of his youthful labors, believes for a moment that the town is still there, alive and present with the imposing ringing of the church bell tower, the symbol of its arms extended towards him to invite him to return to those ruins, to walk those cobbled streets of rounded, well-polished

---

1. *quadra-quadaredda-quadarnni* = large copper pot; small copper pot; large-shaped pot

pebbles, that old square, which was given the name "Elímo" in memory of a distant civilization that is now lost between history and legend, the beloved square where people met, chatted, conversed, establishing relationships of sincere friendship, where the innate need every man has to socialize was fulfilled, to feel alive among people he knows, with whom he could exchange a greeting, a smile. That smile which today, closed as he is within the walls of a house equipped with all the comforts, with marble floors, with beautiful bathrooms and valuable furnishings, he can no longer find; he feels isolated, condemned to pass the days in front of a television and live the last years of his life in a world that does not belong to him, because it is not his world, the one he had the opportunity to appreciate even in hardship and fatigue.

And standing motionless, he watches from the hill above, moved to tears upon seeing that agglomeration of remains and among them he looks for his old house that carries so many dear memories nailed to the walls: he still seems to hear the voices of the women of the neighborhood, the screams of the children who happily played in the streets, the smell of freshly baked bread spreading in the air, the voice of the *gnira*, Mrs. Maria, who looks out the door next to him saying: "*gnira Rosa, mi presta un pani che dumani ci l'arrennu?*" (Can I borrow a loaf of bread that I'll give back to you tomorrow?); the clatter of the mules tied in front of the door of the stable to a special ring fixed to the wall, the chimes of the bells inviting the faithful to pray the Hail Mary; and it seems as if he can hear *gnira* Margherita calling her hens back to the special *"casuzza"*, their house: *cúzzi, cúzzi* or *pii... pii...* and the hens who knew the voice of their mistress, who left the others and returned to their henhouse. And so many other thousand memories crowd his mind: the work, the land, the men, the problems, the trepidations, the drama of every day, the fear of bad weather conditions such as rain, drought, disasters of all kinds, but also the tenacious will to remedy everything, to succeed.

And among all these memories the relationships of life prevail, the expression of passions, the coexistence of solidarity, the relationships between farmers and owners, the love for one's wife and children, the flourishing growth of the girls who convey their beauty and modesty in the simplicity of life; the projection of the life of each one towards communication, the connection to the life of others, the drama, the vital choir that frees voices and sounds around him who like a statue, feels deeply subjugated by the strength of these memories, because they were facts, relationships, men who had filled his past, lived among people who not only knew how to work, but also sing, smile, love with the nagging aspiration to affirm their dignity.

In the homes of the gentlemen, the kitchens were clean with comfortable stoves, while the farmer's domestic hearth was all smoke, soot covering the whole environment, seeming like the forge of a blacksmith. The housewives who lived between the second half of the 19th century and for more than a third of the 20th century did not know the comforts of using a steam cooker made of masonry and covered with decocted tiles, equipped with a charcoal stove and an opening above in concentric iron circles of different sizes depending on the circumference of the pot to be used.

These kitchens were used towards the end of the 1930s, but their spread in the peasant environments came after the end of the war, which in the 1950s followed the use of gas stoves; first alternating with the old fireplace and then the gas stoves completely won out over the use of the old kitchens.

The homes of the rich landowners, on the other hand, were improperly called palaces, because in comparison with the very modest houses of the peasants they had a much more elaborate architectural structure separating themselves from the huts of the miserable. The house was very comfortable and spacious with fairly wide marble stairs, interrupted by landings depicting drawings of various colors and enriched by certain notice boards embedded in the front walls. The entrance was, at least for some of these "palaces," a large door with two halves which led into a large courtyard where the owner's carriage was parked. The stable that housed the horse was located in the back of the house. Most of these environments were in central areas of the town: along Corso Umberto I, near the mother church and the square. And when the rich man passed among the people in the streets of the town on horseback in his fancy saddle, he was respectfully greeted with a "kiss of the hand," accompanied by a bow with any hats in hand. And many years before the Second World War, if the wife of the *burgisi* met a lady on the street with her "Don", i.e., the wife of the rich gentleman, she was reverently greeted with the words "*patruna mia*" or "your servant".

Evidently these forms of reverence have remained in the elderly still carrying traces of servitude transmitted by the previous generations, so much so that in the years that followed the advent of fascism and with the division of some feuds, as well as with the savings of the emigrants, many *burgisi* families became more autonomous and independent, some disengaging from the small feudal lords and others, who could take on larger extensions of land, assumed the burden of continuing the rent or the colony, in a relationship not entirely based on allegiance as in the past, but of mutual convenience; depending on the small property acquired, the colonist gained a different social position in the mentality of the time, deserving of an equally different consideration by the concessionaire, compared to those who possessed nothing.

Photo 6 - Peasant cooking pots

Photo 7 - Kitchen shelf

X - HOME FURNISHINGS

The home furnishings were very simple and modest. The bedroom of the "*burgisi*", that is to say of the peasants who were better off economically, was furnished with a double bed formed by trestles and boards with a headboard and footboard in iron or brass. The mattresses, usually four in number, were stuffed with barley straw or horsehair, but horsehair was already a privilege in itself. The use of wool to cushion mattresses was widespread among the "well off" families.

A chest and a cabinet completed the room's furnishings. The most commonly used chest had a back and rounded sides *(lu cascibanci)*, which left a remote notion of a large sofa for the living room. The cabinet was instead a chest of drawers with a shelf enriched by a slab of white Carrara marble where various trinkets were stored, a dedication to baby Jesus and the husband's clock.

The dining room with adjacent kitchen was just as bare: a rectangular table, necessarily resting on four feet or round with three feet, a cupboard with doors and chairs covered with maguey thread *(zarbarina)* completed the furniture. The furnishings were all quite basic in the kitchen as well: spoons, forks, knives of iron or galvanized metal which deteriorated or rusted over time and were therefore hygienically unsuitable.

From time to time the tin worker that passed through the streets was called on to tin-plate pots and various utensils.

Unfortunately, there were no toilets in the houses because there were no sewer facilities or water pipes. Nor were there cesspools, except in a few houses. For bodily needs, women used a cylindrical terracotta vase, known as *càntero* or *silleta*, or a urinal, while men commonly used the stable. The droppings of the animals in the barns absorbed and transformed all the waste, which was biodegradable in those times: it would be piled up in a corner waiting for the farmer to remove it as manure. To transport it he used a tool made of ampelodesmos fabric that he placed on his mule's packsaddle in the shape of a saddlebag, called *zimmili*. He would empty it in a special composting area in a peripheral part of the town. In fact, these were on the outskirts of some of the main districts: Capo d'acqua, Addolorata, Comune, Convento dei Cappuccini. Anyone needing manure would take it to fertilize their soil. The *borgese* who managed large farms created the composting areas near their premises.

Photo 8 - Chest

Photo 9 - Antique furnishings

XI - THE FAMILY

The family was patriarchal in structure. The father was the head of the family and represented an authoritative figure owed obedience and respect. The same wife and mother of his children called her husband "*vossia*", short for *vossignoria*, meaning your lordship, and the children called their father using the respectful "*assabenedica*" (bless you) whenever he arrived from the countryside or when he left for work. There was a real hierarchy in this first social nucleus: the father was the patriarch, the most authoritative figure in the house; he loved his family and his children but was strict and severe with the latter. He did not dare give them much confidence, but rather uncompromising and demanding obedience and respect. He treasured his life experiences to pass them on to his children, guiding their growth towards the values of precision, thoughtfulness, and wisdom.

The life experiences of the elders codified in mottos, phrases and proverbs were a very interesting cultural heritage, because it helped the formation and behavioral processes of the young.

The internalization of these maxims provided the children of the family with a practical guide of the measures that they had to put in place in the various phases of agricultural work following the teachings of their father, in preventing certain atmospheric phenomena, observing the shapes and movements of the clouds, in using thrift so as not to go beyond the limits of their own availability, *stenni lu pedi, quantu linzólu tèni* (stretch your feet only as far as the sheet reaches); in restraining their tempers, in treating people, in gratitude for the favors received, in using prudence in the face of the equivocal attitudes of people whose sincerity is doubtful. In short, millennial experience that translates into vital teachings for all future generations.

The father was the absolute and undisputed head of the family government; he started the male children at work still at an early age according to the need of the farm he managed; he entrusted them with responsibilities that made a boy an adult at the age which he should have instead been enjoying a playful, carefree childhood.

The woman of the house saw to the needs of the family: she prepared the bread, she took care of the dowry of her daughters for their husbands, she ran the house, ruled over the children, almost by the power of her husband, whom she obeyed and loved even when he did not deserve it.

Photo 10 - Sicilian family and carriage
-52-

To highlight the power of the husband in the patriarchal family, it was said that the Sicilian was gentler with the animals that gave him what he needed to live, than with his family and in particular his children. The facts deny this opinion, because the peasants have always loved their children with a boundless love just as one loves their own blood. In fact, the old people say: "*Li figgu su ljami*" (children are the bonds), and for the children the mother their soul.

A powerful motivating force underlies the entire family: improve economic conditions with sacrifice and work.

The woman sacrificed everything for the sake of her children, followed their development with continuous scrupulousness, apprehension, and anxiety. Usually there were numerous children and in their very early childhood the children needed special care in a destitute living environment due to the lack of adequate hygienic facilities and sufficient and adequate nutrition.

Therefore, the mortality rate of children was high. The bell tolling the death of a child *(la gloriata)*, was heard in the town with a certain frequency. In the poorest families the children would play in the middle of the street, in the dust and excrement of the animals. In summer they could be seen barefoot, and half dressed, their faces dotted with flies attracted by the residues of food that encrusted their face or by excrement, which for lack of thorough cleaning remained stuck to their small bodies.

Hygiene in the families of the "*borgesato*" was more cared for by the housewife's spirit of self-denial, who exploited the miserable existing facilities with zeal, patience, and sacrifice.

Considering the filth that was deposited in the streets due to the presence of chickens, dogs, donkeys, mules and horses, which were continuously transiting there also for the transport of various household goods and supplies of ample consumption for animals and people; also considering the shortage of water, which became precious especially in summer (endless shifts were required for a supply that was barely sufficient to quench their thirst); given that there were no toilets; that large families found housing in homes lacking the necessary spaces, forced to live piled up like canned sardines in certain slums, taking care of cleaning and seeing to the hygiene of each individual and environment required a measure of effort that only the housewives of that time could support.

But the woman not only took care of the children and cleaning the house, she made the bread and this was no easy task either: sieving the flour, kneading it and putting it to rise, in the meantime reaching the proper temperature in the oven with wood to bake the bread *(camiari lu furnu)* and especially feeding the fire in the oven in summer was like bathing in sweat; but the housewife, with

Photo 11 - Woman kneading bread

Photo 12 - Woman taking bread from the oven

her face burned and red, never openly acknowledged her plight; it was there and she endured it in silence and without complaining, taking part of the dough to make pizza with the wood oven that is so appreciated today *(lu cudduruni)*.

The fragrance that emanated from the oven was so enticing that it made the mouth of anyone happening to pass on the road nearby water. It was entirely wholesome: everyone used the flour of their own wheat, which was not poisoned like what we consume today.

The semolina of the flour gave the bread its softness and its particular aroma accompanied its flavor. In fact, it was eaten even for a week and never deteriorated or grew mold.

The housewife would mix the flour to make pasta: a daily task, especially when her husband returned from work every night. She knew how to make different types of pasta: the most common were lasagne, tagliatelle *(li tagghiarini)* and maccheroni *(li maccarruna fatti cu lu bsui)*. Even today, some elderly women make the maccheroni at home; the family celebrates when this happens, because they are a real treat. On holidays and Sundays, possibly when the whole family was together, the most emancipated families of the "*borgesato*" would buy short pasta *(li cavatuna)* or pastina *(la siminsedda)* at the store. But this most likely occurred after the 1920s.

To wash the laundry, the woman used rainwater in winter *(l'acqua gioggia),* which was collected in storage containers from the gutters *(cannaluna)*, while in summer they used spring water, but it was a punishment of God: there was a shortage of water and it required necessary and very heavy, burdensome shifts. There were several sources of water then: that of the "cannoli", the most widely used because in was in the peripheral area closest to the various districts of the town; that of Capo d'acqua used mainly as drinking water, as it was softer than the source of the cannoli. At a certain distance from the village, the water of the springs near the town, "li pili", "la menta", "S. Antoninello", was drawn, but it was necessary to go with animals due to the distance. In fact, the men usually drew the water from these springs. They tied two contraptions called *canceddi* (see photo no. 15) of woven wood, each formed by a pair of cylinders the size of a common terracotta jug, to the packsaddle of a donkey or mule. The load was thus four pitchers and in addition to the connections to the packsaddle, a small pitcher was hung *(quartaredda)* and the cylinder, *lu bummuliddu.*

The water from "cannoli" or Capo d'acqua was usually drawn by the women, mothers and girls. During summer they took shifts putting it in pitchers and had to wait long turns. Rows of jugs could be seen stretching along the

Photo 13 - "Cannoli"

ground, one after the other, in all the adjacent spaces under the scorching sun. It was a mind-blowing sight to see the women scattered here and there, their faces dripping with sweat and perched on the corners of nearby houses to take advantage of the relief of some small, shadowed areas. Often the unnerving wait made them irritable and all it took was a trifle to give rise to what was at times violent turmoil, especially when it degenerated into reciprocal insults and grappling accompanied by the throwing of stones.

When they finally managed to fill their pitchers, they placed the base on their left shoulder and held it in an upright position with their right hand. Then there were the best ones, especially the girls, who could even hold the pitcher straight on top of their heads without needing to use their hands. A truly exceptional test of balance if you consider that the path they faced was sometimes sloped uphill and other times downhill. The girls would put a cotton cloth rolled into a cord on top of their heads, called a *rutedda,* resting the base of the jug on it. Their quick pace, smiling face, fresh and rosy cheeks, thick hair scattered over their shoulders, their narrow hips and the imposing and shapely chests symbolized life in its most explosive youthful fervor, in which reality and fantasy, imagination and hope, aspirations and dreams, impulses of love and secret desires intertwine.

In the summer season it took so much effort to get water that it was not worth using it to wash dirty laundry. And it was customary for the head of the family, when he could afford a day off, to accompany his wife to the river to wash the clothes. More than custom, it was a necessity that lasted until the town established utilities that allowed the homes to have running water. It may not seem true, but for certain needs it was as if time had stopped.

From our first years studying we know that in the *Odyssey*, Homer recounts the meeting of Ulysses with Nausicaa on the island of King Alcinous right at the mouth of a river where the girl had gone with her maids to wash clothes.

To wash the laundry in the home, the women used a *pila,* or washboard, and a wooden tub that was sometimes intended for other uses, including as a bathtub.

In the season in which the tomatoes ripened, the housewife would make and preserve tomato concentrate, quite delicious for meat stew. This product is still made today in some areas of Sicily.

She also took care of procuring all those products that could not be obtained from her husband's work and were considered of primary need: the purchase of potatoes, salt, lettuce, cauliflower, celery, and many other products that the street vendors (such as the famous figure of Uncle Augustine, "*lu zu Ustino*") sold by trading in other products: beans, oats, barley, bran, wheat, eggs, etc. But the housewife's work was not yet complete, as she also collaborated with her husband in the lighter work of the countryside, especially during the periods of more intense work such as harvesting and threshing.

Photo 14 - Crowd at the fountain

Photo 15 - Mule with water jugs

XII - THE FARMER'S WORK

It seems appropriate to include a poem here that focuses on the essential features of a farmer's work.

Un omu 'mmezzu a trazzeri di ciachi Comu lu Signori Ca si trascinava stancu P'essiri 'nchiuvatu a la cruci. Un mulu senza un ciatu di lamentu, Un cani, e intorno silenziu E ciauru di campagna, di montagna.	A man in the midst of pebbles like the Lord who was dragging himself, tired to be nailed to the cross. A mule without complaining, a dog, and all around silence and the smell of the countryside, of the mountains.
'Na visazza... pisanti di na rota di pani di casa, di mezzu ciascu di vinu: la santa comunioni d'ogni jornu e pi cuntornu 'na sarda salata, 'na cipudda...	A saddlebag... heavy with a loaf of bread, with half a flask of wine: holy Communion every day and a salted sardine on the side, an onion...
'Na visazza... vacanti e 'nveci china di tuttu, d'un munnu di rabbia, d'un pugnu di pinseri, d'un lemmi di rigordi.	A saddlebag... empty and instead full of everything, of a world of anger, of a handful of thoughts, of a bucket of memories.
Zappari, arriminari la terra, siminari, abbivirari, aspittari, e poi metiri. Fasci di pagghia, munseddi di frumentu, sacchi di farina... e sapuri di pani. Abbruscari li ristucci, appari ... e 'ncuminciari d'accapu.	To hoe, remove the earth, sow, water, wait, and then reap. Bundles of straw, heaps of wheat, sacks of flour... and the taste of bread. Burn the stubble, hoe... and start all over again.
Un omu, un mulu, un cani, dù visazzi... un disignu a coluri	A man, a mule, a dog, two saddlebags... a colored drawing

supra un pezzu di carta	on a piece of paper
unni si avvicina 'na manu	to which a trembling hand
trimanti ca teni un cirinu	approaches holding a lit match.
addumatu.	
E po..... 'na vampata 'mpruvvisa	And after... a sudden flame and
e tuttu addiventa cinniri,	everything turns to ash, everything
tuttuaddiventa nenti,	becomes nothing,
nenti comu lu ventu..	nothing like the wind.
E lu tempu passa, 'nvecchia e mori!	And time passes, ages, and dies!

Poggioreale currently has an ethnoanthropological museum that is very interesting for anyone who would like to learn about the work equipment and tools of the Poggioreale farmer, which are in fact the tools of the Sicilian farmer with the exception of some typical variants from one province to another.

Thus dedicating pages in this book to describe the form and structure of such tools of labor might seem superfluous and boring, and indeed it is; however, in a book in which peasant civilization is the fundamental topic, I do not think it is entirely out of place to discuss them, also because the more testimony we leave, the more we ensure their memory when faced with events, linked to man or not, that could destroy every trace of their existence.

In the previous pages we have already mentioned the hard life that the work of the countryside required at the time, carried out with the help of animal strength and the sturdy arms of the worker. It was also mentioned that the work was focused on survival; there were no great demands for the future, nor were they urged by the continuous and exhausting desire to change.

This static existence did not urge the farmer to modernize the use of the land, passing from extensive to intensive crops.

Hence until mechanical means gradually replaced the strength of animals, in our area we continued cultivating grains: wheat, beans, oats, barley, etc., with the exception of the small plots of land that served and are still a crown around the town. These were cultivated in olive groves and partly for the production of seasonal fruit for the family, meaning some pears, apples, plums, pomegranates, almonds, figs, prickly pears, walnuts and cherries. These scattered trees also included some orange and lemon trees. There were no actual orange groves or citrus groves in the area of Poggioreale, except for a few small plots belonging to the wealthy.

The basic economy was fed by the production of wheat, which offered the means of subsistence not only to producers, but to the whole community: shoemakers, carpenters, masons, tailors, blacksmiths, small traders, day laborers and owners.

For the peasant Poggiorealese, the land was in their blood and flesh, more than in their brain. When they talked, they always talked about the land, the fertility or lack thereof in the soil, the agreement of contracts with the landowners, the vintage year, the harvest, the weather conditions.

The work of the farmer knew no interruptions or periods of rest, except those to which he was obliged due to rainy days, which sometimes lasted for weeks and weeks, even compromising the work of sowing in the appropriate season.

XIII - SOWING

This was the work rite with which the peasant entrusted the seed to the land, invoking the blessing of God.

Usually after the first autumnal rains, he would plow the land to make it loose. Before sowing he would plow it again *(rifunniri)* to crush the larger clods *(li timpuna)* and finally sow the seeds.

On the subject of sowing, a poem by our fellow citizen and teacher Gaetano Zummo deserves to be included. He received flattering recognition of his talents as a poet in Italian and especially in Sicilian dialect in the competitions in which he participated. In fact, the poem that I have the pleasure to include in this book was worthy of being included together with others he wrote in an anthological collection of poems by Sicilian authors entitled *Petali di sole*[1]. He was also awarded second place in section A of the "Altofonte" poetry prize with the lyric poem "Bagliore di nuova luce" (Flash of new light) in July 2001, and third place in the sixth regional prize for poetry and fiction with the story about the drama of Cudduredda, a little girl from Gibellina who fell victim to the 1968 earthquake.

The poem bears the title *Lu pilu russu,* which in our dialect identifies the red color of the cattle of the so-called Modican breed in Sicily.

The poem thus interprets the work of sowing:

'Mpaiati vannu li voi di lu campu a la vers lu capizzagghiu a li corna e lu mussu tirami lentu l'aratu chi spacca la terra allupata di verdura; hannu li naschi aperti, la testa vascia, lu pi	The paired oxen go down the field in the right direction, tied at the muzzle and horns They slowly pull the plow that splits the earth full of weeds; their nostrils flared, their heads low, their hair red.
La vommara affunna 'nta la terra modda, sbota la timpa chi subitu fumia; l'aria è fridda assai e pari 'na badda 'nfacci, la matina prestu quannu nivarria.	The plowshare sinks into the soft earth, turns over the sod that immediately releases steam; the air is very cold and feels like a snowball to the face when it snows in the morning.

[1] *Petali di Sole* (Petals of Sun) edited by Giacomo Bonagiuso and Francesca Incandela, Mazzotta publisher, Castelvetrano, 1999.

Lu viddanu è chinu di speranza e di vogghia anchi si sapi chi l'astaciuni è ancora luntana e la so testa scura ci cummogghia 'na birritta virdi fatta di lana.	The farmer is full of desire and hope even though he knows summer is still far away and he covers his dark head with a green woolen cap.
Ci pinnulia 'na coffa di la spadda, e' attaccata cu 'na grossa pastura, di furmentu 'ni teni tri munnedda, e ci scinni a lu ciancu, davanti la cintura.	From his shoulder hangs a basket attached with a thick rope with six kilos of grain descending from his side, ending in front of his belt.
La coffa iddu rapi cu la manu manca e cu la ritta pigghia la semenza. La spargi a mezza luna e 'nun si stanca e prea e spera nni la provvidenza.	He opens the basket with his left hand and with his right takes the grain. He scatters it with his hand drawing a half moon, not tiring, and prays and hopes for divine providence.
Lu so gestu è largu e sapienti Lu so passu è cadenzatu e lentu, arriulatu da un rimtu custanti, jetta ad ogni sbraccio un pugnu di furmentu.	The gesture of his hand is broad and expert His step is cadenced and slow, regulated by a steady rhythm, with each movement of his arm he throws a fistful of wheat.
Lu furmentu, vulannu di lu pugnu, luci nill'aria comu faiddi d'oru; Lu brav'omo pensa chi 'nta giugnu, a lu so postu attruverà un tesoru.	Flying from his fist, the wheat glistens in the air like sparks of gold; the good man thinks that in June, he will find a treasure in its place.
Lu siminaturi avanza lentu lentu, li pedi pisanti di crita, grossi comu na vastedda, aisannu la testa ora è chiù cuntentu e talia la chianura larga e bedda	The sower advances slowly, his boots weighed down with earth as thick as bread, raising his head now he is more contented in looking at the large and well cultivated countryside
'lluminata da un suli giannuffeddu chi cumparennu però la negghia spapura e mannannu nterra lo so calureddu li manu quadia e lu corpu tuttu accalura.	Lit by the somewhat yellow sun that overlooks the fog and evaporates, giving off a faint warmth that warms his hands and body.
Pi cummigghiari sti coccia di furmentu, 'mpaiati vanno li voi attaccati pilu mussu, tiranu l'aratu adagio adagio, a passu lentu, li naschi aperti, la testa vascia, lu pilu russu.	To cover the grains of wheat, the paired oxen tied at the muzzle pull the plow slowly, slowly, their nostrils flared, their heads low, their hair red.

Plowing was still carried out with the ancient and millennial nail plow in the shape of an open S, which had the iron plowshare *(vòmmara)* wedged in the lower flap. The oblique section had an opening where the lower end of a beam *(percia)* was lodged, about three meters long, whose angle was adjusted by a wedge-shaped piece of wood called a *cúgnu*. The upper part of the plow was molded into a grip *(manuzza)* to allow the farmer to adjust the furrows in the soil. The other tools for pairing the mules, *'mpàiari*, were: the yoke, *lu iùvu,* another wooden rod shaped with grooves made in the support points on the bearings; the pads, *li pannèddi,* were made of olona (thick cotton fabric) or leather, padded with straw and attached to the wooden arches on which the yoke rested after they had been placed around the animals' neck. The *percia* had holes at the upper end for attaching to the yoke by means of a ring and a special nail. The different holes were used to adjust the angle of the plow.

The pair of mules or oxen were guided by two ropes that connected the halter, *lu tistàli,* of the animals with the grip of the plow, or *manùzza* (see photo no. 17).

Once the animals were paired up, the plowing began. Whenever the plow became filled with soft earth, the operator cleaned it with an iron paddle attached to a wooden handle, called *varvùscia.*

The day was long, and the work was very hard. The breaks for eating meals allowed a slight repose for the weary limbs of both the animals and the farmers. They ate breakfast in the morning, lunch at midday and an afternoon snack. At each stop the farmer first took care of feeding the animals: he would put a certain amount of beans and oats, *pruvènna,* in special bags of olona *(lu sacconi)* and tie them to the head of each animal after introducing their snout. The animals subjected to this very onerous work had to be fed well if a satisfactory yield was to be achieved.

Then the farmer would go to sit "*a li róbbi*", the place where he had left the saddlebags with his own food and that of the animals, take out what his wife had very carefully prepared for him (a jar containing black olives or crushed olives seasoned with oil, vinegar and garlic, a piece of bread, some pieces of pecorino cheese) and would have breakfast. Meanwhile, he would realize that he had not fed the dog wandering around, stop his meal for a moment, take the bran bread from his saddlebag specially packaged by his wife for the dogs, and give it to them.

Finally, after seeing to the animals, he could eat his simple, modest

Photo 16 - Wooden plow

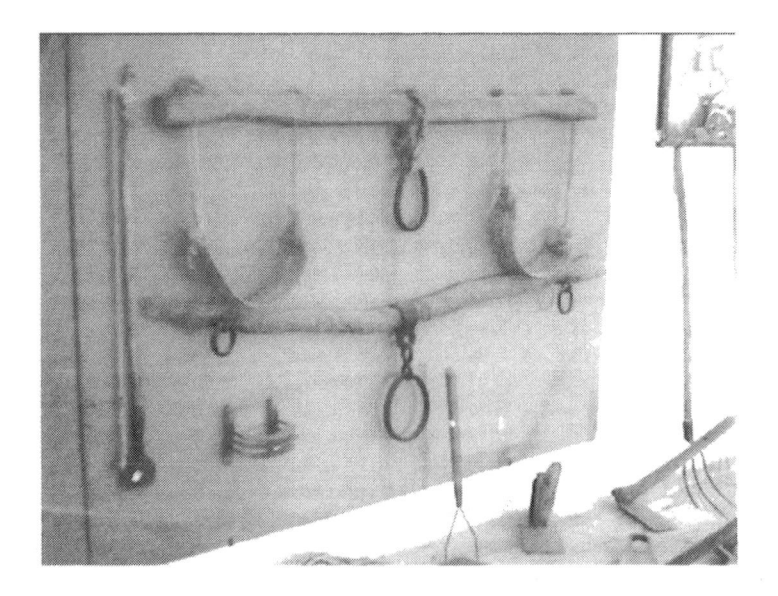

Photo 17 - Rod-yoke for pairing the mules

95

Photo 18 - Plowing
-69-

breakfast. Yet he certainly enjoyed that piece of bread and cheese; possibly awake since four in the morning and urged by hunger, he would devour his frugal breakfast with a real appetite. And above all he would be serene, calmly observing the sun every now and then to understand the time of day. He would turn his gaze from time to time to the plowed earth which had an acrid and wild scent, and was pleased with the work carried out.

These were small satisfactions, but for those who were attached to the earth, for those who did not know other relations in work and life, if not those that were and constituted their own world, their emotional ties, the satisfactions were feelings that arose from simple things: from the beautiful day that allowed them to work uninterrupted, from the wild landscape at whose center he saw himself as the main protagonist in a life lived outdoors, where the mules ate the *pruvènna,* snorting inside the bags, where whirling around in the air, the birds seemed to cheer up nature with their singing, while others soared closer to the ground in search of the insects moving among the clods, where the dog serving as a guard *a li ròbbi,* making his presence known by barking, as if it also felt pleasure in festively inserting itself in that mysterious choir of voices which rise in the air, almost to dissipate the sense of sadness that nature, shabby and cold, instills in the heart of each man.

This is how a poem in dialect by Vito Oliveri renders these moments in the life of the farmer:-70-

A passu passu 'ntra la matinata, e 'ngruppa di l'amicu muliceddu, tantu cu lu suli forti o malutempu, 'ncampagna si nni va lu viddaneddu.	At a slow pace in the morning, riding the mule and friend, whether there's a strong sun or bad weather in the countryside, the farmer sets off.
Canta biatu nni ddu regnu amicu, cci vivi filici e po' sunnari, dda trova paci comu 'm paradisu, dda tutti l'amarizzi po' scurdari.	He sings blessedly in that friendly kingdom, he is happy there and can dream, there he finds peace as in Paradise, there all bitterness can be forgotten.
Canta di cori e dannu zapponati, la frunti si cci jnchi di suduri, e sunnu gocci d'acqua biniditta, chi vagna dda terra e la 'nsapura.	He sings heartily, even though he hits his hoof, his forehead fills with sweat, and they are drops of holy water, which bathe the earth and flavor it.
L' ariddu mattinieri lu saluta, 'a farfalledda 'nfacci l'accarizza, vola l'acidduzzu e cci fa festa,	The morning cricket greets him, the butterfly caresses his face, the small bird flies and celebrates him,

la campagna ridi d'alligriza. Chiddu chi nasci è vera biddizza, 'u frumminteddu è d'oru culuritu,'a verdura, l'arancio, 'u piriddu, soccu metti 'n mucca è sapuritu.	the countryside laughs with joy. What is born is true beauty, the wheat is colorful gold, the vegetables, the orange, the pear, everything put in your mouth is tasty.
Oh! 'ngiusta suciità chi nun cumprenni L'omu di campagna e nun l'apprezzi, lu sfrutti e pri lu cchiù cu rancori lu chiami viddanu e lu disprezzi.	Oh! Unfair society that does not understand the country man and does not appreciate him, exploiting him and moreover with resentment you call him a villain and despise him.
Si cumannari putissi 'na jurnata, stu munnu tantu 'ngratu e tantu duru, all 'omu di campagna un munumentu, e tuttu d'oru, cci lu facissi puru.	If I could one day command a monument in this ungrateful, hard-won world for the country man, and all of gold, I would certainly do it.

In the sowing season the days would often grow damp and cold, the Tramontana wind from the north would grow sharp and penetrate between the limbs of the body exhausted by fatigue, but the farmer would not give up, continuing his work unperturbed, not even when a slight drizzle *assuppa viddanu,* making the work more tiring due to the softened clods that would stick to his feet, to the hooves of the animals and to the plowshare that required continuous cleaning with the *varvuscia*[1].

His feet were protected by sturdy boots manufactured by the shoemaker, and his legs were protected by *burzacchini* or *plantari* (they were called boots if they were made of leather, *plantari* if they were made of waxed canvas tied to the legs by a cord of hemp *(rumaneddu))*, but it was also true that he was exposed to humidity and the risk of developing bronchitis that could even become chronic and stay with him for a lifetime. A ragged velvet jacket would cover his shoulders and a pair of *d'intoccu* pants covered his legs, perhaps with patches at the knees and the bottom. They would always make the most of a garment before retiring it. And the housewife spent long hours patching up various garments of the family.

When the rains were continuous the farmer would rest, spending long hours observing the weather, feeding the animals, or repairing work equipment at the blacksmith, who during the sowing period was the craftsman he visited the most frequently to put shoes on the mules and restore his many tools used daily.

---

1. Varvuscia = iron harness in the shape of a paddle with a wooden stick used to clean the plowshre of the soft earth stuck to it.

Photo 19 - Break from sowing for breakfast

Meanwhile, the housewife would prepare a hot, steaming soup of country vegetables in the kitchen: chicory, wild fennel, very common in our area, or chard *(giri),* borage, *cavuliceddi.* On rainy days she frequently prepared a hot dish of fava beans cooked with various vegetables which, accompanied by a few glasses of wine, was nourishing for the whole family, aimed at chastening the harshness of the first cold of the late autumn season.

Then in the evening, in the hours of rest, a great brazier full of live embers, with all the members of the family gathered around its warmth, almost as if to symbolize the ancient and mythical domestic hearth, the central node of the blood bond, from which spontaneously arises, without any preconceived forcing of customs, the character of the indissolubility of the first nucleus of man's social life.

It was a time of family warmth, during which they conversed with simplicity and modesty, the conversation always revolving around the facts of the day; perhaps they gossiped about a neighbor's behavior, the way this or that girl was dressed, the shrewd looks of the young girls in the church with local young men, the sicknesses pervading the town, people who had passed away, accidents with mules and horses, future prospects and a great deal of other news which, passing from one mouth to another, spread throughout the town with the speed of a communication on television.

However, the gossip was not prompted by feelings of envy or animosity or by the need to vent hatred towards people who do not seem kind in the eyes of those who are pleased to gossip, but by feelings of friendship, of human drive towards the person to whom we want to feel close, even by criticizing their work.

It may seem absurd that talking about others could be an expression of affection and friendship; but this is how it was, at least for those who did it with a sincere soul, with honesty, and without personal grudges.

In the autumn season wine was made by those who owned plots of vineyards. This task was entrusted to the carpenters, who would go to the customer with special equipment to transform the wine.

The blacksmiths worked at full speed, forging the iron, beating it on the anvil to shape it into the object they had in mind to create. And they were real artists, because without the help of the machines that we have today, they managed to create items of exceptional skill using only the blows of a club and a hammer on the anvil.

They worked late into the night to complete the work scheduled for the day. The cadenced beats of the club on the anvil resounded among the streets

Photo 20 - Brazier
-74-

of the town, mingling with the noise of the carpenter's saw, with the blows of the shoemaker's hammer, with the chatter of the people who met in the streets, with the pawing of horses and mules, making sparks with their hooves in the cobbled streets washed by frequent rains. The rinsing from washing the animals near the "cannoli" area was joined in unison with the hustle and bustle of the *trappeti* (oil stone mills) for milling the olives.

It was a symphony of noises, voices, barking dogs, bells on goats and sheep, the braying of mules and donkeys, the traffic noise of carriages returning from their daily work, the exchange of greetings, the ringing of bells announcing the first hour of the evening: an intensity and vivacity of life that made the inhabitants sure they were not alone, giving them a feeling of well-being, of comfort, of participation in the life of the community, in the midst of which the very reason for their lives found meaning.

The sowing continued and sometimes lasted almost all of December. The temperature dropped to low levels, and it was often necessary to stop working; the earth would become muddy, the peasant tracks difficult to travel.

In the farmhouses where the cultivation of grains was complemented by breeding sheep and cattle, the hired men were exposed to bad weather, to the cold wind, the rain, to the storms that pervaded the mountains and hills on particular days. And the poor shepherd who knows nothing but the countryside and his sheep lives far from the world of men, wrapped in waxed canvas and protected by a bag of sheep's skin and fuzzy pants.

These poor "devils" suffered long periods of solitude and would see the town and their family every once in a while, according to the agreements set with the master.

'U pastureddu by V. Oliveri

A deci o novi anni su jttati
a la vintura, 'n tra munti e
vadduna, cu lu friddu o la calura
di la 'stati, mmenzu li pecuriddi e
li muntuna.

Quann'è la sira, stanchi e
strapazzati, pri ddu misteri faticusu
e 'ncuttu; hanno 'i piduzzi unci,
scarcagnati, 'nta la panzudda sulu
pani aciuttu.

And when they were nine and ten,
they were thrown into the midst of the
mountains and valleys,
in the cold or in the heat of summer,
in the midst of sheep and rams.

When evening comes, tired and worn out
for their hard and assiduous job;
their feet swollen, kicked,
only dry bread in their stomachs.

E criscianu accussì, comu l'armali,	And they grew like the animals,
senza canusciri nenti di stu munnu,	without knowing anything of this world,
socch'è chi fa lu beni e fa lu mali, li	what it is that does good and does evil,
gioi e li dulura chi cci sunnu.	the joys and sorrows that are there.
Si fannu granni, arrassu di la genti,	They grow up far from the people,
luntanu di la matri e di lu patri, suli,	far from their mother and father, alone,
'n compagnia di fami e stenti,	in the company of hunger and hardship,
assicutati di lupazza e ladri.	targeted by wolves and thieves.
Diventanu omini abbunazzati, comu	They become quiet men, like
fraticeddi di cunventu, o comu	friars of a convent, or like
picureddi appena nati,	newly born sheep,
chi tremanu di lu scrusciu di lu ventu.	who tremble at the blowing of the wind.
Chiovi ed è notti, 'u picurareddu sta	It rains and it's night, the shepherd is alone between the mountains and the
sulu 'ntra li munti e li vadduna,	valleys, poor boy, who makes his bed with a
poviru figghiuzzu, cu lu scialliteddu	shawl
si fa lu lettu e talia la luna.	and watches the moon.

The persistent rainfall often interrupted the work of the day workers, so they often asked the *borgese* for some wheat to feed their family and with the promise to return the favor with work on days when the weather was good.

In this period, once the olive harvest was over, the farmers saw to milling the olives at the local mills. In Poggioreale there were three to four oil mills of ancient and archaic form between the two World Wars: a hard stone mill rotating on a circular base. The driving force was that of animals: a blindfolded donkey was connected with the axle of the grinding wheel by straps and various harnesses; it was forced to walk around the circular base where the olives had been placed. As it turned, it pushed the axis of the grinding wheel forward which slowly moved and crushed the olives into paste, while the water and oil flowed into a vat through a special groove.

The separation of the oil from the water was usually the task of the housewife, who removed the oil with a plate with skill and caution. Once the oil was collected in a cask or another container, it was stored in the home in enameled terracotta jars, which are still used today.

The olive paste was stuffed into special baskets woven with resilient fiber, *la curina*, and was exploited as much as was possible by the presses. These were operated with the brute force of the workers' arms, *trappitara*. In fact, a solid beam axis equipped with arms in the shape of a cross was connected to the press by a thick hemp rope. Four workers, two for each arm of the cross, operated the press by rotating the cross, and each turn was accompanied by the cry of the workers who harmonized their work in chorus, shouting: *O... ooh forza! oh, forza!* while the donkey, with the monotonous and continuous ringing of the bell, communicated his moans and gasps that evaporated in the air of the mill, impregnated with the acrid smell of the pomace and the sparkling fragrance of the freshly extracted oil.

When the paste was dry it was deposited in a corner, then used in winter as charcoal to keep the embers in the brazier lit for a long time. The *trappitata*, or milling, lasted a long time and required shifts because they worked 24 hours a day.

After the oil was harvested, the *borgesi* resumed the work of sowing. This was carried out by scattering *(spagghiu)* the seed for a more even distribution, the plow was used to delimit the *brocia,* meaning the strip of land that was precisely wide enough to be included in the scattering of wheat that the farmer withdrew from time to time from his basket, the *coffa,* filling his strong fist. The most commonly used seeds were "*lu bilì*", "*lu gianti russu*", "*la biancolidda*" and "*tumminia.*"

The latter was usually sown in January, when the sowing season was greatly extended due to bad weather.

When the grains of wheat grew green in the fields in spring, the weeds were uprooted. A long narrow long hoe, the *zappudda,* was used for this task in order to avoid accidentally cutting the stalk of wheat together with the weeds.

The women also helped carry out the weeding work, *zappuliari,* when the wheat became tall, they removed the weeds directly with their hands. When rain made the soil soft and it would stick to the hoe, the farmer would clean it with an iron tool tied at his waist called the *rasòla.*

And in the meantime, the continuity of the work was never interrupted, because once full spring was upon them, the farmer had to reap the clover for the animals' hay. The tool he used was a large scythe called a *fullana,* whose handle had a double grip to allow gripping it with both hands. The tool was heavy and each swathe required the use of all the strength of his arms; in fact, working the long hours of the day to harvest the hay was a grim job. In the evening the farmer's back would certainly feel it, his arms falling weak at his sides. The rest of the night relaxed him and helped him reset to resume the onerous work the following day.

The cut grass remained stretched out on the ground to dry under the rays of the sun and then, no later than the beginning of the wheat harvest, it was tied in bundles and transported to special barns. At the same time the farmer was busy laying out the *favata* in the sun for drying as well, meaning the seedlings laden with fruit, before threshing them. Thus, it was a relentless job that very often even stole a few hours of nightly rest from the farmer. And he could not complete the above-mentioned work, which stole time away from the approaching moment for harvesting the wheat.

XIV - THE HARVEST

With the first ten days of June, immediately after the feast of the patron saint of Poggioreale, St. Anthony of Padua, the farmer's most intense work began: the so-called *staciunata*.

The harvest season had arrived, which set the farmer to long, back-breaking work, which he however faced completely willingly, with true devotion and a spirit of sacrifice, standing tall and reinforced by the hope of being rewarded for the efforts suffered during very long and endless months.

Just like in sports competitions where the athletes put all their resources to work to reach the final goal in a dignified manner, so the farmer devoted the utmost of his energies in the hopes that the final goal could repay him for his worries, his uncertainties about the weather conditions, the hardships, the exposure to cold, *furtura,* and bad weather and lastly the continuous and persistent worries to ensure that he and his family could enjoy a certain economic tranquility, even if limited to the bare necessities for survival.

"Giugno, la falce in pugno!" This is the expression used in the past in the first days of June, meaning, "Take up your sickle in June!". In Poggioreale, as in other towns with a purely agricultural economy, there was an influx of seasonal immigration at the start of this month.

They were internal migratory flows which moved from the cities of the neighboring areas to the countryside, where the demand for labor was more pressing at the beginning of the harvest.

So already from the first days of the month, many daily workers moved to the country waiting to be hired.

Poorly dressed, with a shoulder bag, a blanket, and some modest provisions, they found shelter in the open space in front of the Church delle Anime Sante (Armisanti) located in Piazza Elimo in front of Corso Umberto I.

Bored and tired during the day, you saw them sitting on the sidewalks or seeking the shelter of some tiny shadow that the houses projected at the corners of the streets; at night they stretched out their blankets and laid down next to each other, like many soldiers camped out in the open. If in the late evening some of the "*borgesi*" approached, many stood up in silence, expressing their exasperated anxiety to be chosen with their eyes alone.

Photo 21 - Havesters at work
-80-

The most depressing and mortifying scene of all was the choice of the number of workers needed. The employer, as if he were reviewing military fighters, carefully examined each worker from head to toe, eliminating the older ones, those who seemed physically fragile, choosing the younger ones, the more robust and those whose physical presence appeared of indubitable strength.

These were humiliating scenes that severely offended a man's personal dignity and left traces of indignation in anyone who had a minimal amount of sensitivity and awareness of human rights.

The implorations of the workers who realized they were being cast aside were translated into phrases like: "Hire me, please! Put me to the test, please! I'll be as good at the work as the others. Do it out of charity, for my children who have no bread at the table!"

Others instead walked away silently without uttering a word, their faces deeply marked by the mortification, resting their backs on the corner of a street, their eyes absent, their souls shaken. And many of those passed over, once the hirings had ended, returned home in a beaten-down state of abandonment of every initiative, hoping only for the help of providence.

The crew of hired workers was accompanied to the *antu,* the workplace where the harvest was started. Before starting, the reapers would take some precautions to avoid getting hurt with the sickle. In fact, many wore a reed thimble on their middle finger and ring finger: these were the fingers most likely to be cut by the sickle. Some workers wore *lu vrazzali*, a sleeve of resistant fabric to protect their arms from the ears' rubbing while working. Others wore a sturdy olona apron, *lu pitturali,* to parry unexpected hits from the sickle.

Thus the harvest began.

When the worker's hand could no longer contain the harvested bundle *(jermitu),* he put it on the ground. Usually six to eight workers worked on the *antu,* who were followed by another worker, often the owner of the farm, who expertly tied the bundles *(lu liatúri)* into sheaves. The bundler carried the ties made of ampelodesmus at his waist *(li ljàmi ddi ddisa),* which he had already prepared in bunches in the spring season. To bind the bundles in sheaves, the binder used an iron hook called *ancineddu* and a wooden hairpin called an *ancina.* He used the iron hook to push many bundles into the wooden hairpin, as much as it could contain, laid out the ampelodesmus tie on the ground and placed them on it; he repeated the same step until he formed a sheaf *('na règna)* that he tied tightly. All day long the "binder" had to follow behind the reapers:

Photo 22 - Packsaddle with saddle and saddlebags

Photo 23 - Mules with packsaddle

he had to be physically strong, fast and have a lot of skill; in short, it was a specialized job that not everyone could do, and was quite tough.

If the harvesting work was stressful because the reapers had to work under the hot sun of the month of June and with their backs bent from sunrise to sunset, the work of the binder was even more exhausting, who had to collect the bundles left here and there by the reapers in a bath of sweat from morning to night.

The sweat solidified in whitish spots on the workers' faces like layers of salt and a pitcher with water was continuously passed among the various thirsty mouths to restore the body with some of the liquids it had lost.

The only repose they had was when they stopped to eat meals. Indeed, they took five breaks during the day to eat, some longer and others shorter.

The meals were usually eaten at the *ántu* and started at seven o'clock in the morning. The menu was quite meager and changed depending on the farm, but was more nourishing than in the other work periods. Very roughly, simply to provide an idea, at seven o'clock in the morning after half an hour of work, the workers were given some bread and cheese; breakfast was given around nine o'clock and consisted of a plate of potato stew with eggs, so-called *agghiotta*.

Around one in the afternoon they had lunch, which was their longest break *(la scuddata)*, which consisted of offering the workers an abundant plate of pasta with sauce; at about five in the afternoon they had a snack consisting of meatballs with potatoes, then lastly in the evening a snack consisting of bread and cheese. This daily menu was one of the best, because in some farms the dishes were much more meager.

In the large farms, one person was in charge of preparing the daily meals, while in smaller farms the farmer's wife took care of everything. Wine was also offered during these meals, passed around in a flask to be shared. At the end of each break the workers resumed their work, protecting themselves from the sun which on certain days of the scirocco would even break up stones, using straw hats with wide brims and continuously quenching their thirst with water. But when the wind ceased and the air became sultry and hard to breathe, at times some of the workers less tempered to endure such slaughtering work would collapse at the *antu,* suddenly fainting. The work in those days did not last eight hours as today, but from dawn to dusk and it was therefore necessary to be accustomed and well hardened to bear such heavy burdens

At the end of the day the sheaves were placed in groups of six, as many as could be loaded onto the packsaddles of the pack animals: known as *s 'incavaddavunu*[1], meaning they would form *li cavaddùnghi*. In the evening the workers, with their foreheads encrusted with sweat, the edges of their mouths smeared in white like the foam that settles on the bite of the horses, would lie down on the stubble, always in the area of the *antu*.

During this period many families would move to the farm to collaborate with the men, at least in the preparation of meals for the workers. Once the harvest was over the day workers were dismissed, unless there was a need to retain some to continue some work related to the *staciunàta;* while in the larger farms their collaboration continued with annual or monthly wages.

The sheaves were left to cure for the entire harvesting period. Then the threshing floor was prepared for threshing the grain.

---

[1] *S 'incavaddavunu* = arranging the sheaves on the ground, three on one side and three on the other, ready to be loaded on the horse's packsaddle. The set of six sheaves was called *cavaddunghiu*.

XV - "LA STRAVULIÀTA"[1] AND THRESHING

This was the name given to the transport of the sheaves on the back of mules to the threshing yard. The work required the help of efficient workers, because they were forced to stand from morning, possibly before dawn, until sunset and were subject to the continuous consumption of energy: loading the groups of six sheaves on each animal was quite a physical task, also because it consisted of continuous loading and unloading all day long. Another worker was stationed at the threshing yard with the task of arranging the various sheaves in a pyramid, the *timugna,* to protect them from any rain before they were threshed, but above all to occupy little space and facilitate their transport to the threshing yard when the time came.

The choice of the threshing yard's location had to meet certain requirements, mainly including good exposure to the winds of the mountain or the west, then the nature of the ground which must not be subject to landslides during the winter, to avoid continuous movements of the yard from one year to another. The first step was to level the ground after delimiting the circumference of the yard, which for a pair of mules was about ten, twelve meters in diameter. Then they went on eliminating any cracks by filling them with a soil hoe and a lot of water, *acquari,* and in order to make the soil compact and beaten down, a lot of straw was spread together with the water.

Having prepared the threshing yard, the tied sheaves were arranged around the yard to avoid scattering the ears during the *pisata*. Lastly, the untied sheaves were scattered in the yard and when the sun warmed them for a few hours, usually around nine in the morning, the threshing began, making the mules beat their hooves on the sheaves scattered in the yard.

60 to 80 sheaves *(regni)* were placed in the threshing yard for each *pisata*, that is, from three to four larger sheaves, *mazza di gregni*. The innermost animal, guided by the *pisaturi* with the reins, was indicated with the expression *la mula di li manu,* while the other that walked outside was called *a lu firrìu*. The animals were paired by the farmer according to the yield that the animal could have given.

The animal that stood *a lu firrìu* had to cover a larger path and be faster than the one inside.

---

1 *Stravuliata* = transport of the sheaves into the threshing yard on the packsaddles of the animals.

Photo 24 - Transport of the sheaves into the threshing yard

The circular trot of the animals was followed by the movement of the man who urged them on with some whipping and with voices and styles that traditions had codified and transmitted from generation to generation. Every now and then the rotation was reversed, first to obtain a better crushing of the sheathes, and then perhaps to prevent the animals from becoming dizzy.

Then when the upper layer of the sheaves was already reduced to straw, the underlying bunches not completely crushed by the hooves of the mules were removed; the mules were led outside the threshing yard and the workers used a trident to overturn the threshing yard *(vutavano l'raia)*. Then the threshing was continued until the straw was minutely crushed.

During "*la pisata*" of the workers with the trident, they continued to throw any ears that ended up outside the circle back inside. The *pisata* lasted four-five hours. It was a very tiring job that the farmer faced at a good pace, striving to transmit his good mood also to the animals that collaborated with him under the solicitations of the whip and the songs urging them to keep the rhythm of the trot constant in this hard work they were subjected to. Below are some verses of the dirges sung by the farmer:

Allegri muli e cuntentu cacciaturi	Cheerful mules and happy farmer
Chi v'è dari 'na bedda nova!	that I have good news to give you!
Mina lu ventu e arrifrisca!	The wind blows and softens the heat!
Tu va a lu ventue gnè a lu riventu	You will enjoy the fresh wind and I the rest
Aduramu e ringraziamu lu sant.mo	we adore and thank the holy
E divinissimo sacramentu.	and most divine sacrament.
Batti e ribatti	Back and forth
Cu l'aria si cummatti	in the threshing yard we work
E cummattemu, cummattemu Fino a	And we trot, we trot
quannu la pagghia facemu.	until we make straw.
Tagghia e ritagghia Chi	Cut and cut again
l'am 'a fari pagghia	because we must make straw,
Chi po' mina lu ventu e si la pigghia.	that after the wind threatens and carries away.
Arriventa la spadduzza	You find rest by going the other way,
Chi t'abbenta la tistuzza	so you won't get dizzy
Accussi arriventu eu	so I also rest
Accussi arrivanta lu cumpagnu meu. E	as does my partner.
arriventamu tutti, o cori meu!	And we all rest, my heart!

Arriventa e arriventamo	Lie down and we'll lie down
E a Gesù e Marita chiamamu	before Jesus and Mary we call
E chiamamu ad ogni istanti	them at every moment and we
Puru l'Angili e li Santi.	also call the Angels and Saints.
San Marcuzzu, minati lu ventu!	St. Marcuccio, threaten the wind!
Evviva lu Santissimu Sacramentu!	Long live the Blessed Sacrament!
Viva la Madonna e lu Signori,	Long live Our Lady and the Lord,
dati forza e valia asti poveri muli.	give these poor mules strength and endurance.
Santu Nicola, Santu Nicola,	Saint Nicholas, Saint Nicholas,
beddu lu suli , bedda la parola!	Beautiful sunshine, beautiful word!
Fòra , fòra , li muliceddi fòra!	Out, out, the *"muliceddi"* out!

    These songs capture the farmer's hope of a good harvest, and thanks to the Lord, putting his worries and hard labors into those blond ears beaten by the hooves of the animals. The final exclamation "Long live our Lady and the Lord, give these poor mules strength!" symbolizes the deep fellowship between man and the work animals; the term of endearment *"muliceddi"* almost expresses an image of the perfect symbiosis between two individuals of different species.

    St. Nicholas was invoked to communicate that the end of the *pisata* had come: "Saint Nicholas, beautiful sunshine, beautiful word! Out, out, the muliceddi out".

    The mules would leave the threshing yard dripping with sweat, which would dry up and leave white crust on their skin.

    The men would also leave the yard for a few hours with their faces dotted with straw attached to the sweat.

    The housewife would make sure their midday meal was ready: hot pasta with simple sauce or with meat stew; sometimes instead of pasta they were given a first course of potatoes, zucchini, eggplant, flavored with various sauces and enriched with eggs, which were given as a second course.

    Lunch was consumed at the edge of the threshing yard if the main house or haystack was far away.

    The meal was always accompanied by a flask of good, natural wine. When the great pot was uncovered with the steaming pasta and a particularly inviting scent was released, the children's appetite was most pressingly stirred, all of them eagerly staring at the pot waiting to be served; the priority was given to

Photo 25 - Overturning

Photo 26 - Overturning

the husband and the men who rested on the ground, taking a short rest before resuming the work that awaited them.

Once the meal was consumed, the men waited for the wind to rise to separate the straw from the wheat *(spagghiari)*. In fact, as soon as the wind could be felt *('mmurca lu ventu)*, the overturning began: the straw was lifted in the air with the wooden trident and the wind would carry it to a margin of the threshing yard, forming a half-moon shape *(la margunata)*.

In order to prevent the annoying straw from penetrating the belt of their pants, causing redness or itching, the men would pull the lower flap of their shirt outside their pants so that it covered the sides.

The overturning was also a tedious job: sometimes the straw sent into the air with the trident, under the thrust of wind blowing in the opposite direction, was thrown into the workers' faces and bodies together with the grains of dust that blinded their eyes.

In fact, when the *spagghiari* was finished, the men would go search out water to clean themselves, their faces sprinkled with sweat and smeared with dust and straw.

And so, day after day the same work was carried out: the threshing and the separation of the straw from the wheat until all the sheaves of the *timugna* were finished.

Once the threshing was completed, the grain was cleaned and divided into three phases:

1) the *paliata,* meaning the lifting of the wheat in the air with a wooden shovel to free it of the small bits of remaining straw. The man holding the shovel was preceded by another worker who used a narrow trident to remove the wheat to facilitate the work of the *paliari*, that is, to allow the "*paliaturi*" to fill his shovel more easily.

Pushed by the wind, the straw was deposited in the area in front of the *margunata,* forming a smaller heap called a *bastarda* or *ciusca*. In the end the wheat was collected in piles in the center of the threshing yard and the farmer was already able to estimate the amount of the harvest. Using the trident backwards, he sank its handle into the center of the pile of wheat, measuring the fold with the palm of his hand, *cu la gnutticatura,* the part which was buried, and calculating the consistency of the pile in salmas.

2) First sorting with the wide-meshed sieve which allowed the wheat to pass through and instead retained the grains that hadn't been shelled, *li gruppa;* these were set aside and shelled with a wooden tool called *mazza*.

The sieve was called *crivu d'aria* and a tripod was needed to use it, built by the same farmer with maguey beams, called *zarbara*. The big sieve hanging in the middle of the tripod by ropes was sent back and forth by the smaller sieve for sorting the grain.

3) The sorting with the narrow-meshed sieve, *lu crivu d'occhiu,* which did not let the wheat pass and sent down the traces of earth and fine grains that had not matured, *lu scagghiu.*

Photo 27 - Threshing yard sieves for various sizes for grains

XVI - TRANSPORTING THE WHEAT
"LA CARRIATA DI LU FURMÈNTU"

Once the cleaning was completed, the wheat could finally be transported home. In the meantime, it should be borne in mind that certain debts were paid with the wheat directly on site. In fact, some of the craftsmen who had provided the "*borgese*" with equipment and various kinds of work would visit the various yards during the threshing to receive their payment in wheat. The blacksmith above all would bring his accounts ("ferula matrice") in which he had indicated the prices of each job he had carried out, marked in notches on a rope in his workshop; after his accounts were compared with the other part *(figlia)* kept by the farmer, he was paid for the work he had carried out throughout the year.

Some shoemakers and barbers sought their payment as the blacksmith did. Others instead waited for the farmer himself to pay his debts contracted during the year. And before the wheat of the pile was bagged, there were also other offers to satisfy: the remuneration to certain people who had helped work during the year. There was no shortage of religious contributions either. The monks of Tagliavia would also go around collecting the offerings.

They arrived with imposing, well-fed mules and usually received a generous offer ranging from four *tumoli*[1] to a half *salma* of wheat depending on the farm's availability.

La carriata di lu furmèntu, or transport of the wheat, was then completed on mule back along paths of scarce quality. However, in summer these tracks were ignored and summer paths were followed which, in addition to being easier, allowed to shorten the distance between the countryside and the town.

Each mule carried eight *tumoli* of wheat, about 250 pounds, distributed with four in a saddlebag called a *visazzotta* and four in another called *visazza*. The first was made of olona in the shape of a large saddle and tied like a normal harness on the back of the mules, the other (*visazza*) straddled the first, with the two bags hanging on both sides.

---

[1] A *Tumolo* or *tomolo* is a wooden, cylindrical tool used to measure grains (wheat, barley, oats, etc.), which can contain about 30 pounds of wheat. Besides the *tumolo*, the following were used: the decaliter (35 lb of wheat); the *munneddu,* equal to 1/4 of the *tumolo*; the *quartigghia,* equal to one fourth of the *munneddu.*

Depending on the availability of mules, rows of two, three, four mules traveling from the countryside to the village were used to transport the wheat. The large farms had a "*rètina*" composed of nine mules. Each mule had a crownpiece with a bow hanging from its face with many bells at the bottom, which rang as it passed through the streets. The most beautiful mule rode at the head of the "*rètina*", ridden by the guide who was called the *vurdunàro*. Within the farm, the *vurdùnaro* mainly worked with the animals; he knew their defects and habits, according to which he chose them for jobs.

La carriata di lu furmèntu was shorter or longer depending on the farm and demonstrated the diligence and endurance of the farmer, who already exhausted after a long season of intense work, must continue to sleep little at night and endure the continuous physical effort to load and unload the saddlebags from the back of the mules. Already at three o'clock in the morning he would have to start preparing the animals for loading and then transport.

The streets, the paths, the countryside tracks were full of these rows of mules, whose continuous braying was covered by the jingling of the bells and the singing of the farmer, who would sing old love songs to drive away the boredom of the journey that made him sleepy, its echo lost in the silence of the night.

The entire countryside was full of people. There were those travelling from the town to reach an area of the countryside, those who were transporting the wheat, blacksmiths riding mules to visit the threshing yards and receive payment for the work they had carried out, women who would bring the children to the farms where their husbands worked, gleaners who would wander the fields under the sun in the frantic search for ears of wheat left among the stubble.

The countryside was an exultation of life: the weeping of children, the distant voice of the wives collaborating with their husbands, engaged day and night in their intense work, the bleating of sheep, the bellowing of cattle, the singing of the larks, the cry of the shepherds leading flocks through the fields, all voices that rise and are lost in the air to signify the fervor of life animating the countryside in this period.

The harvest period infuses a note of gaiety in the soul of the farmer and his family, because finally after a year of hard work, he can pay the debts he has accumulated with the shoemaker, the carpenter, the barber, the bricklayer and other craftsmen. However, some years were unprofitable due to adverse weather conditions; then all this fervor was lacking because the harvest was not enough to pay all the debts and help the family avoid a life of hardships.

The harvest season was completed with the transport of the straw home;

in addition to being a fundamental food for the animals, it had many other uses: to light the fire, to heat the oven for making bread, to fill the mattresses, make the stable dry, etc. A large wide-mesh net called *ritùni* was the tool used by the farmer to transport straw. He filled two nets with straw and laid them upon the packsaddle of the mules. In addition to being bulky, the full nets were very heavy. The farmer had to have strong arms and be practical when loading them, that is, he had to balance them well so that along the way, with the movement of the animals sometimes travelling uphill and other times downhill, they would not shift and become uncomfortable for the animal who was already agitated due to the heavy load and suffocating heat.

During the hottest hours with the sun striking down on them, the dust would rise from the paths due to the passage of the animals, the straw sticking to their faces, suffocating their breath and making the journey unbearable even for the farmers who were most hardened and tempered to a hard working life.

These large bales of straw were emptied into special haystacks where the children often enjoyed beating it to make it more compact, helping to make more space in the room.

And so the *staciunàta* came to an end and the men working the countryside could finally rest, tormented by a stressful and exhausting job, whose daily duration for the owner of the farm and his adult relatives was not from dawn to dusk, but from a few hours before dawn to late in the evening.

When I say rest, I do not mean that he rested without any commitments until autumn, I mean that his work became less tiresome compared to the summer period.

The harvest can be said to end the agricultural year. The "*borgesi*" also owned some plots of vineyards. The districts where the vineyards were more widespread, including fringed trees, were the *dagali* (flat lands) and some hilly areas near the town. The most common grape variety was *caterratto,* the harvest of which was carried out in October. Small amounts of grapes were harvested, enough to produce wine for family needs, with the exception of some families whose vineyard holdings were larger.

The harvest brought a cheerful note to the vineyards. It was carried out above all by the women, among whom young girls prevailed, brightening the air and the surrounding environments with their festive singing, with their easy laughter, with that youthful euphoria that raises hymns to the life that beats strongly inside their chest, full of future promises.

The harvested grapes were deposited on a canvas and then collected in baskets of woven reeds carried on the back of mules to the home for crushing. When seeing the farmer pass with a load of grapes, the children would abandon their games and run behind him asking for a bunch of grapes: "Avvossia, mi duna un sganchiddu di racina?" (Sir, can I have a bunch of grapes?).

At the end of the harvest the grapes were crushed using ancient methods, as in the times of Ulysses in the cave of Polyphemus.

A worker or the same farmer would step into the tub of the grape press and press the grapes with his feet until the must was completely squeezed from the stalk. The must was then poured into special barrels, already prepared in advance to receive the grape juice.

XVII - FOLKLORE AND FESTIVALS

In 1846, English scholars were debating about the name to be given to a people's knowledge, *Popular antiquities*. In the literary magazine "Athenaeum," the archaeologist Ambrogio Merton (1803- 1885) proposed using the word "folklore," a term coined using the two words folk= people and lore = knowledge. This term began to be used to indicate the knowledge of a people, but also the science that deals with it.

Thus, the word folklore spread internationally and was adopted, replacing the Italian use of the expression "popular traditions" (*tradizioni popolari*).

Folklore is therefore the study of the traditional life of a people, mainly attracting the interest of artists and writers following the decline of humanistic classicism, as a discovery of the world of the humble. Initially this interest manifested itself as simple curiosity, because the scholars had no awareness of any studies. This curiosity in the 18th and 19th centuries opened the way to the work of erudition and ontological research that would become real science.

In Italy the founders of the science of folklore include Vico for some parts of his *Scienza Nuova,* L.A. Muratore for his works *Antiquitates italianae* and *De Superstitione vitanda,* Tommaseo for the great collection of popular *Tuscan, Illyrian, Greek Songs,* but the most productive advocate between the 19th and 20th centuries was Giuseppe Pitrè (1841-1916), who decidedly boosted folklore to give it its definitive position in the scientific field. Thanks to him, the daily life of the small-town people of cities such as street vendors, storytellers, and charlatans, and of villages such as shepherds, peasants, and village and rural people emerged within the ranks of science.

The manifestations of folklore can be indicated using the words of the same Pitrè: "Fairy tales and fables, tales and legends, proverbs and mottos, songs and melodies, enigmas and riddles, shows and parties, traditions and customs, rituals and ceremonies, practices, beliefs, and superstitions, a whole open and hidden world of reality and imagination moves, is stirred, smiles, whispers to those who know how to approach and understand it."

With its peculiar condition of predominantly peasant people and craftsmen living in traditional rural culture, like all the populations of agricultural environments, the Poggiorealese people have passed through a dense web of traditional customs that motivated the actions and situations of which their existence was woven.

The manifestations of Poggiorealese folklore can mainly be seen in the religious festivals. Religiousness instilled that sense of serene acceptance of an uncomfortable life in our people which, in the months and seasons that followed each other, took place between traditional patterns of festivals and customs that were in tune with the rhythms of nature and the agricultural work. In fact, beliefs and customs reflect the forms of culture and magical and religious conceptions typical of a life lived in more immediate contact with nature, regulated according to its laws and according to the interpretation of its phenomena. And although the religious sense of life has changed over time, the customs linked to the unchanging course of the seasons have remained without completely losing the characters and aspects that had allowed them to arise and be handed down.

Confirming the religiosity of the Poggiorealese, it is enough to mention a passage from the book *Memorie Storiche di Poggioreale* (Historical memories of Poggioreale) by Arch. N. Caronna which states: "Faith is grafted onto the soul, and more than anything else, lives in the very simple and innocent breasts of the children of the people. And in those days, better than in other times, it beat in the heart of principles. As well as a center of life and healthy culture, religion was the first breath of life here, and the small shrine welcomed the first heartbeats of our ancestors, of those poor children of the field."

In addition, the presence of the numerous churches that were built over time and the numerous priests who worked in the small village are testimony of its lively religiosity. Therefore, religious festivals were very popular and included the participation of the entire population, without distinction of age. The state of destitution, the uncertainty of the future, poverty and misery, the daily exposure to diseases due to hygiene and healthcare shortcomings, the frequent cases of typhus, the relentless malaria that afflicted a large part of the active population, kept families in a constant state of anxiety, apprehension, fear for which they found liberation and comfort in faith in God, Almighty Father, in the hoped-for grace of the Lord and of the Saints.

And the priests, in the past more than in the present, were called on to carry out their priestly functions according to a relationship of trusting and comfortable mediation between the divine and the human.

The priest gave comfort; his friendly word encouraged hope, offered relief from despair, pointed to the way of the Lord and the reward for suffering and adversity.

Robust and rigorous moral conduct was rooted in this religious background, whose observance framed the manifestations of life within patterns which, while clashing with the urges of the heart and the spontaneous demands of human nature, were accepted as a deterrent to perdition and sin.

The festivities that were most appreciated in Poggioreale with lively appreciation and enthusiasm were and still are today Christmas, New Year, Carnival, St. Joseph, and above all that celebrated in honor of St. Anthony of Padua, the town's protector and patron saint.

XVIII - HOLY CHRISTMAS

This holiday was anticipated by every family. The Christmas atmosphere began to emanate from the day that the *novenas*[1] were celebrated in the church in the early morning, with the ample participation of the faithful. These prayers then culminated in the solemn holiday of the night of Christmas.

The Mother Church was full of people who celebrated the holiday with an open, emotional heart. It was not the Christmas of today where the spirit of the holiday is mystified by the culture of consumption, by the glitz of shop decorations, by the flickering of the lights revealing richness and grandeur in the streets and squares. These new customs transform the holiday into a pretentious occasion of consumerism and easy gains and not into an occasion of rebirth of life, regenerated by the religious fervor that awakens in the souls of all with renewed intensity, when the notes of the organ accompany "Tu scendi dalle stelle..." (Italian Christmas carol written in 1732), sung by the crowd in church and propagated in all the homes by the ringing of bronzes, announcing the birth of Baby Jesus at midnight. Groups of children moved among the columns of the church, giving the ceremony that guise of naivety and innocence, that outline of educational incisiveness, which widely benefited all present, both big and small.

Moreover, observing those children who at the time of the Baby's arrival stood on tiptoes, eyes towards the High Altar with their breath suspended waiting to hear the outcome, was a source of emotion, because you could see the solemnity imprinted on those innocent faces that opened their hearts to the love and joy that comes precisely from love.

Then there's the small nativity scenes that the mothers prepared with care and dedication at home for their young children. It was not a sterile, empty reconstruction aimed at reproducing the scene of the birth of Jesus in a stable as realistically as possible, but a profuse reproduction of noble feelings of faith. The passion and love with which the mothers arranged the nativity scene highlighted the most immediate messages that it transmitted directly in the children's eyes: the feeling of love that strengthens the affectionate relations

---

1. *Novena,* from the Latin "novem", indicating a cycle of prayers lasting about nine days for the celebration of Holy Christmas.

of the family union and that we understand without fearing an incorrect interpretation, in the image of the Madonna and of St. Joseph lovingly bent over Baby Jesus, this sign of the paternal and maternal bond that unites them to their own creature; the spirit of brotherhood, symbolized by the presence of characters of different social order who humbly kneel in the presence of the child prodigy.

Today these messages are no longer so clear, but on the other hand the nativity scenes, empty of meaning, are full of characters, artistically modeled statuettes, various animals that seem real, rivulets and lights of various colors embellish the scene, distorting the tradition of poor St. Joseph and altering the original symbols, in the sense that the nativity scene has become a scenic reconstruction without a soul, like a mannequin of a beautiful showcase.

The bond then of the indissolubility of the family, symbolized by the nativity scene, is reflected in the custom of still considering the anniversary as the feast that unites the family around its table. In fact, the motto: "Natale con i tuoi e Pasqua con chi vuoi" (Christmas with your relatives and Easter with whoever you like) is quite significant. And if even today in Poggioreale many emigrants face long and uncomfortable journeys to spend the holiday with their relatives and their families of origin at Christmas, think how much the need to spend the holiday with relatives was originally felt back then. Siblings and their families were reunited with their father and mother, lavish feasts were prepared with special dishes for the holiday, including the turkey that the housewife had raised with care for the Christmas table, the desserts that the women had prepared according to tradition with real dedication (the *buccellati* cookies filled with ground dried figs).

The spirit that animated the holiday was imprinted in the strength of family ties and in the acceptance of the values that the family possesses, as the first nucleus of an established society.

Today the family is in crisis. Economic well-being, the means of mass communication, the revolutionization of values, the need to live life more freely, the rejection of the strictness of certain customs, the result of pre-established family education, the need to leave room for the pleasures of the table, sex, entertainment, and sometimes transgressive pleasures, have shattered a lifestyle that was based on simplicity, modesty, and unsuffering resignation.

XIX - NEW YEAR

The customs of the Poggiorealese in celebrating the start of the new year were no different than in the other towns in the area and in southern Italy. In reality, Christmas, New Year, and the Epiphany are all holidays that solemnize the end of an annual cycle and the start of a new one. Thus many of the rites and customs resemble each other despite the diversity of the general conditions of the various environments in which the same customs take place.

In Poggioreale, the new year was celebrated in the family as at Christmas: the ceremony in the church and a large meal full of particular, special dishes. With several families of relatives all at the same table, cheerfully enjoying more elaborate and abundant foods on the first day of the year was also a reason to forget arguments, calamities, and misfortunes. In fact, according to certain beliefs, participating in the holiday in a climate of satisfaction, joy, exhilarating pleasure, is a good omen to keep certain social and economic malaises or other hardships at bay. Even then many families waited for the new year to come between a dish of fried cardoons and a few bites of homemade sausage, accompanied by the requisite glass of good wine, celebrating the entrance of the new year with rifle shots into the air, the sparkling of firecrackers, and hugs full of good wishes. They did not throw away old furnishings, because they only possessed what was in the house, but the custom of shooting at the old year was felt, because it was connected to a very specific purpose: to eliminate, erase, destroy all the evils, the troubles of the year passing and wishing for abundance, well-being, and prosperity in the year to come. Thus the aim was to destroy the evils that had passed, physical and moral evils, infirmity, to face the new year healthy and with wishes for the perennial resumption of the seasons of the new year. Therefore, always in relation to the principle of sympathetic magic and to spread certain omens, it was necessary to avoid becoming restless, sad, request payments, while joy and the exchange of good wishes were the conditions for a peaceful year to come. The omens to recall include that of the calends, according to which the atmospheric conditions of the first twelve days forecast, by analogy or opposites, the weather that would come in the twelve months of the year. The meteorological omens had a role of primary importance for the entire Poggiorealese community.

XX - CARNIVAL

This was another festivity, which although it was not religious, offered the poor souls an opportunity to relax, free from daily fatigue and nagging worries, in which despite the humiliating conditions of life, they allowed themselves two days of jubilation and joy.

Banquets were organized for this holiday as well, full of meat and various delicacies and evenings full of dance, cheered by the sounds of the guitar and mandolin. It was another opportunity for everyone to sit at the same table among families linked by close kinship, or for the families of young people who had become engaged to join together.

The term "*carnilivari (livari carni)*" reflects the etymology of the Latin word "carnem levare." And this is what led to the custom of enriching the banquet with meat dishes, among which stewed pork stuffed with garlic, pepper and other the spicy ingredients that flavored it reigned supreme, along with grilled sausages that were exquisite, especially thanks to the genuineness of the meat, because it came from animals fed foods that were equally natural. Today it is impossible to find such flavors due to the breeding systems, thanks to the sophisticated resources of the industry oriented towards the highest possible yield. Today the rational breeding systems of meat intended for consumption and for the most immediate earnings place meat from select animals on the market, which are beautiful and flashy to the eye but tasteless and sometimes nauseating to the palate.

The holiday also includes different ceremonies and traditions today depending on the regions and towns where the celebrations are held.

In some places in France it begins at Christmas, in others with the New Year, in some places in southern Italy and Sicily it begins with the Epiphany. In Poggioreale, Carnival was held on the three days Sunday, Monday and Tuesday before Ash Wednesday, although many families observed Fat Thursday as the beginning of the festival. The last day of Carnival celebrations is the Fat Tuesday that precedes, as we know, the period of Lent during which leaner foods are eaten.

At that time the use of masks was very widespread, especially among the young and very young. There were no masked balls in the town, nor did they sing special Carnival songs, but many families held dances in their homes. The front door remained open to allow masked guests to enter, enjoy some dancing and leave. When entering, one of the masked guests would make themselves known to the man of the house to avoid any unpleasant surprises. Groups or pairs of masked people would run among the cobblestones and muddy streets, making the atmosphere festive with the ringing of bells or loud chimes. As is still the case today, the masks depicted heads of animals, fearful snouts, images of beautiful 18th-century damsels and women's faces, and devils who recalled certain pre-Christian rites.

There were none of the masked balls as are held today, with flashy displays of clothes and elegance, where ladies and gentlemen show off their glitz and glamour, testifying to the state of well-being of many families.

It was a modest way of celebrating Carnival, because the people of the town were modest and spontaneous, without the ambition of mimicking the typical lifestyles of the highest classes in their snobbery or freeing themselves of the inferiority complex that many young people suffer today. The celebration was for everyone: young people, teenagers, young and old. Considering that the dances were held in the family, the elderly participated and truly enjoyed the party perhaps with a note of nostalgia for their youth, when they were young and beautiful and held secret thoughts of love, not without some perceptible sign of modesty and shamefulness.

The whole family's participation in the party avoided any marginalization issues among its members (the elderly or children), harmonized emotional bonds and balanced relationships.

Today a new ethic rules relationships within the family, as the habits of life have changed. Well-being has made the forms of distraction and fun more and more refined; the parties require larger spaces for the pleasures of life and therefore children and the elderly are again excluded: the former are entrusted to babysitters for the occasion, the latter are no longer around the home because the custom of nursing homes has become widespread even in smaller towns. The figure of the housewife of the past no longer exists, it has disappeared with the peasant society, and caretaking elderly parents at home is also disappearing with the latter, and in many cases this happens in the towns not because the mother of the young family works, but because the old constitute a constraint that is no longer reconcilable with the new needs of life; thus it is more convenient to pass the elderly on to the responsible institutions. Certain prejudices on the basis of which it was once a shame to send parents to nursing homes have been overtaken by a more evolved mentality that is more in line with the tendency to live life more freely, not suffocated by various restrictions and constraints.

Following the calendar, another traditionally celebrated festivity, and more in the past than in the present, was that of St. Joseph. This recurrence is no longer considered a holiday in calendars, nor in schools.

XXI - ST. JOSEPH

This holiday was very celebrated by the population and was deeply felt within the soul, with a frankness of sentiments and a spirit of religiosity. Recourse to the help of the Saints was frequent and was motivated, as has been mentioned in the previous pages, by the sufferings due to the precariousness of living, to the frequent epidemics, etc. The Patriarch St. Joseph was invoked in the most critical moments of need, regardless of the reason. And the invocation, carried out with ardor and with all the strength of feeling, was always accompanied by the solemnly advocated vow: the offering of an altar full of gifts for the poor.

The preparations began a long time before the holiday. The families interested in fulfilling the vow were very zealous, keeping fruit beyond its season and all kinds of delicacies, which they used to enrich the altar. The more sought-after the objects and gifts to be exhibited were, the more prestige their vow acquired and the more it was believed to be accepted.

Often the preparation of the altar was like a contest among the women of the neighborhood, who together with their relatives would work hard to prepare dishes and desserts.

Patience, love, and religiosity required the women to prepare for the holiday with long days of work. Among the preparations, the cakes of St. Joseph deserve mention. They consisted of three enormous *buccellati* (cookies) weighing more than four and half pounds each, which represented the most significant offer of the vow, others were instead smaller and were presented in various shapes of palms, sticks, hearts and so on. The preparation of these cakes, a tradition that is still maintained, was quite particular because the dough was kneaded *(scanata)* and worked for a very long time to make it firmer.

Among the various preparations, an exclusive and I'd say also artistic tradition of Poggioreale took on particular importance: making the *squartucciato*. *Squartucciato* are sweets depicting sacred objects and made with two sheets of kneaded dough with a thin layer of ground dried figs in the middle. The sheets were shaped like a heart, a monstrance, palm, cross, St. Joseph's cane, but the most demanding job that required skill and application, as well as imagination and creativity, were the carvings on the upper layer of

Photo 28 - Women working on the squartucciato

139

Photo 29 - Examples of squartucciato
-109-

Photo 30 - Altar of St. Joseph

the sheet, which like precious embroidery, depicted twigs adorned with beautiful flowers and images of angels symbolizing the sacredness of the altar. In fact, the heart symbolizes the heart of Jesus in whose center, always by carving, are the initials G.M.G., those of Jesus, Mary and Joseph in Italian. The center of the Monstrance had the initials J.H.S. The cross symbolizes the cross of martyrdom which, at the end of the meal offered to the poor, is given to the child representing Jesus for the occasion.

The palm on the altar symbolizes the purity and virginity of Mary; the flowers on the cane represent the holiness of St. Joseph; the peacock is the distinctive recognition of the Christians in the period of persecution. As can be seen in the photo here, the finely carved desserts highlighted the sumptuousness of the altar and suggested not so much the idea of their destination for consumption, but the great intensity of faith and the votive spirit of the population of Poggioreale.

The decorations were also quite rich: the laurel at the sides of the altar, the abundance of breads, the variety of flowers, the variety of sweets such as cannoli, *fritelle, (sfingi),* sfogliatelle *(cassateddi),* different size cakes of ricotta and cream, *pignoccate* together with the multiple variety of fritattas made with wild fennel, asparagus, artichokes, broccoli, eggs and potatoes, placed among trays of all kinds of fruit and delicacies, all creating an altar full of majesty and grandeur to arouse admiration, curiosity, and interest in the visitors who came and went from one altar to another. It can be said that on the eve of the festivity all the people of the town crowded the streets to visit the altars, both to oblige an invitation received, and for curiosity and devotion.

The visitors, together with the people who offered the altar as their vow, sang propitiatory songs to the Saint, reciting hymns and chanting in vernacular in an atmosphere of spirituality and heartfelt devotion. Among these hymns and chants, below are some passages of a composition written in the early 1900s by a Poggiorealese poet, Giovanni Palazzotto, and a villager, Vincenzo Fazzino, recited from memory before the few altars that are still built:

O summu patriarca gluriusu, specchiu di santità e di allegru visu, patri di l'arma nostra ginirusu, patruni siti di lu Paradisu.	Oh glorious high patriarch, mirror of holiness and cheerful countenance, father of our generous soul, Master of Paradise.
Lu piccaturi nni mori cunfusu, chi si 'ni penti d'avirivi offisu; pirdunatilu vui patri amumsu, chi di tuttul'arcanu siti 'ntisu.	The sinner dies confused, for he repents having offended you; forgive him, loving father, for you have heard of all the arcane.

Siti 'ntisu di tuttu l'arcanu, chi siti Patri di lu Nazzarenu e patri ancora di ogni cristianu, d'ogni piccaturi c'avi frenu.	You are heard by the whole arcane, because you are the father of Jesus Nazarene, and the father of every Christian, of every sinner who has faith.

Patri di la Provvidenza Vi chiamamu,
       'nta tutti li bisogni a Vui
       curremu, in fini di la
       morti, Vi priamu
e assistitini Vui in ogni puntu estremu.
Di li pochi pitanzi chi truvamu
Nui oggi a pranzu vostru li mittemu,
lu 19 Marzu v'ammitamu.
	Father of Providence we call you,
	in all needs we implore you,
	and at the end of death we pray to you:
	assist us, at every extreme moment.
	We put the few dishes that we find
	today at your lunch, and
	on March 19 we invite you.

E Vi ammitamu cu pani ed aranci Cu pignulati, cassateddri e sfingi, di diversi pitanzi ed autri ranci d'ogni poviru divotu chi si stringi.	And we invite you with bread and oranges, with *pignoccate, panserotti* and *sfingi*, with different dishes and other foods that every poor devotee can offer.
L'addavuru vi uffremu pi l'oduri Chi lu truvati 'nta qualunque artaru, balacu binidittu ed autri ciuri, chi su 'na meravigghia di guardari.	The laurel we offer you for the odor that you find in any altar, blessed wallflower and other flowers, that are a wonder to look at.
Mennuli e nuci cu li scorci duri, li soli petri li ponno scacciari cussì è lu cori di lu piccaturi, chi Vui sulu putiti arrimuddari.	Almonds, walnuts with their hard shell, I know that stones can crush, thus is the heart of the sinner, that I know only you can soften.
O piccaturi di tuttu cà attornu, tu chi bestemmi d'estati e d'immernu ammita S. Giuseppe a lu so jornu avi lu Paradisu in eternu.	Oh sinner in the surroundings, you who blaspheme in summer and winter, invite St. Joseph on his day, he has Paradise forever.

On the morning of the festivity, the priest would visit all the altars and consecrate them with holy water. The ritual of inviting the poor to lunch, who embodied the three characters of the sacred family for the occasion - Jesus, Joseph, and Mary - took place at noon. Before lunch, the hostess together with the other women of the family would perform some additional ceremonies: they knelt before the three boys *(li santuzzi),* renewed the ritual of washing their feet, drying them, and lastly kissing them. At the end of the ceremony, the lunch began: first the pasta of St. Joseph was served, a dish which according to tradition had to be made with simple and inexpensive ingredients, a symbol of poverty and simplicity which was not so simple if you consider that the dish was seasoned with a sauce of tomato concentrate and enriched with the addition of rice, very good wild fennel, beans, and stewed broccoli. In short, it was so good that even today it is considered a delicious dish and, it can be said that for the anniversary of the feast the traditional dish of St. Joseph is still served on all the families' tables.

The first course was followed by the other courses consisting of a taste of all the fried dishes and all the sweets and delicacies that had been displayed on the altar. At the end of each ceremony the three poor boys each received a large *buccellato* (cookie) as a gift, were dismissed, and sent home. In addition, a taste of all the delicacies and treats enriching the altar was offered, by devotion, to friends, relatives, and all the families of the neighborhood.

The customs of this feast suggest a heritage of timeless values, founded on love and the spirit of solidarity.

Among the messages that the festivity immediately puts before us, the following should be noted:

- the religious spirit that has a positive impact on the manifestations of human life by limiting the excesses of selfishness, hatred, hypocrisy, and the exploitation of others;
- the social value that unites the people of small towns like a large family; in fact, the holiday allows families to meet, strengthens their relationships, offers an opportunity to commensurate with others, distances the aspects of isolation, and allows the dialogue that nurtures feelings;
- love for thy neighbor inherent in offering bread to the poor. This ritual conveys a deep meaning of love. The vow that the people promise and that materializes in the creation of an altar does not have a value in itself, but that of charity towards those who suffer from hunger. This is the motivation of the offering in the promise of the vow, in the name of St. Joseph, father of Providence, of bread, sweets, fruit, and various delicacies, to those children who lived a poor, wretched life.

The intensity of the devotional fervor that accompanied the motivations for the offerings can be seen in some songs, hymns, and litanies that were sung and recited with passion before the altar, as can be deduced from passages such as this: "Patriarca immaculatu / Di Gesù custode amatu / castu sposu di Maria/ prutiggiti l'arma mia. / Giuseppe Santu... / spusu e guardianu di Maria / la grazia chi vi dumannu / concessa mi sia." (Immaculate Patriarch / Beloved guardian of Jesus / chaste spouse of Mary / Protect my soul. / Holy Joseph / Husband and guardian of Mary / May the grace I ask of you / be granted.)

The holiday was so much more felt and celebrated than it is today, conveying noble messages that must be protected and not forgotten. Indeed, it is necessary to recognize the "Pro loco" tourist association of Poggioreale, chaired by Cav. Nicolò Tamburello, the commitment with which it has worked to solemnize the festivity every year and therefore perpetuate its tradition with the creation of a large and sumptuous altar in honor of the Saint, at the same time highlighting the prerogative of the *squartucciato* in the eyes of the villagers and tourists. Interesting exhibitions have even been organized that focus precisely on highlighting a tradition that rightly deserves a project to enhance the prestigious and artistic carving work that the women knew and still know how to create in a special type of dessert, precisely called *dolci di* S. *Giuseppe* (St. Joseph's sweets).

They embody imaginative embroidery that cannot fail to attract the wonder and attention of even the most distracted observer. The hope is that the "Pro loco" association can continue to solemnize the holiday, so that those to come can continue to appreciate a tradition that conveys valuable messages and not only for this, but also because it represented, in an era in which the human rights of our ancestors were undermined by the anguish and suppressed by the ruling class, an opportunity to rediscover the comfort in faith, where the pain of suffering could be dissolved.

XXII - THE FESTIVITY OF ST. ANTHONY OF PADUA

And finally, the holiday with the largest, warmest, most intense and profound participation of all the Poggiorealese was and is dedicated to St. Anthony of Padua, patron saint and protector of Poggioreale.

Devotion to the Saint is in the blood of the Poggiorealese, it is in the most intimate fibers of the soul. When speaking of the origins of the town, Arch. Nunzio Caronna[1] wrote: "Religion was the first breath of life here, and the small shrine erected east of the castle, with the title of St. Anthony of Padua, welcomed the first heartbeats of our ancestors." This expression leads to some reflection: a simple proposition but full of sentiment, affective impulse, of respect for our ancestors, towards those humble, modest men who fought, who faced discomfort and suffering in accepting life, projected in the hope of tomorrow and in the intervention of Providence.

The mention of their "heartbeats" is incisive and penetrating, it is the fulcrum of the entire expression within which Caronna has summarized the complex world through the life of a community of people, which is the people of our origins. The entire affective world that moves and operates in the daily life of a population is summed up in this one word, that is, the heartbeats, the palpitations, aspirations, upheavals, tremors, and stirrings and above all the deep breath of courage and tenacity in which the worries and restlessness of conscience find rest. And finally, the use of the possessive pronoun - our - before ancestors gives the expression an immediate effect of the attitude of reverence that pulsates throughout the sentence.

St. Anthony is invoked as the miraculous Saint and the true protector of all the Poggiorealese. The Protector's help was invoked on every occasion of need: diseases that put the lives of family members at risk, in long periods of drought or in long rainy seasons and in many other forms of calamities and tribulations. As mentioned before, devotion is in the bosoms of all and is not induced by the emergence of a state of need. The invocations for help were surrogate to the promises of the vow, consisting, as we know, in following the entire path of the procession in his honor on bare feet and carrying lit candles;

---

[1] Arch. Nunzio Caronna, *Memorie storiche di Poggioreale,* (Historic Memories of Poggioreale) Ed. G. Gianfala, Palermo, 1901.

but offers were also made in money, aimed at making the festivity as solemn as possible. On the contrary, it is superfluous to specify that the offers in cash to support the organization of the festivity were given by all the families of the town according to the availability of each and with deeply felt participation.

The festivity was organized by a committee led by a chairman who, in advance, assumed the burden of collecting offers by passing among the various houses. In the past, much of the offerings were made in nature and the committee visited with well-saddled mules to transport the wheat. Today the festivity is organized much less elaborately than in the past, when in addition to horse racing, the holiday was enjoyed with a much deeper satisfaction. In fact, the holiday took on different tones and was noticeably felt for two fundamental reasons: the first was given by the strident contrast between the everyday way of life of the peasant families, full of deprivation and hard work on the one hand, and the longed-for rest, enlivened by the festive atmosphere that spread in the streets of the town on the other; the second reason lies in man's instinct to appreciate distractions and diversions all the more intensely, the more exasperated his deprivation in the daily process of life. Thus the lack of these distractions, the rare opportunity to meet especially among the young people or to wear new clothes and show them off in the streets where the party was being held, the strict observance of certain behaviors and habits that were lived as restrictive and oppressive and the impulses that stir within, can lead to a more explosive enjoyment of the celebration. It allowed the inhabitants to go out and watch horse races, walk in the square and along the main road to visit the fairgrounds and to allow themselves the opportunity to buy various furnishings, to breathe in a different atmosphere than the daily one they were so accustomed to.

The notes of pleasure and gaiety enjoyed with full participation were therefore more incisive than today, where the youth more frequently have fun and enjoy entertainment which is not linked to the celebration of religious holidays, where celebrations are not attended in order to be able to enjoy elaborate meals; on the contrary, very strict diets are recommended to combat diseases due to the excessive consumption of calories.

It was all an exuberance of festive events, supported by the numerous presence of *semai* who would set up stands in the various corners of the square to sell nuts, peanuts, roasted pumpkin seeds, and the famous white and colorful *torrone* (nougat), well as the presence of many toy stands and those selling equipment for domestic and farming work.

Attracted by the toys, the children and youth would pass from one stand to another to buy something with the money they had received for the occasion from their parents, grandparents, and closest relatives. Even the cart of the man selling colored water was always surrounded by children who had fun drinking bottles of water of different colors.

The stirring of the people that crowded the square and the main street, the influx of families from the nearby towns of Salaparuta and Gibellina, the shooting of firecrackers, the band that gathered crowds around the so-called stage to listen to songs of classical music or other popular works, the deafening roar of the drums, the fireworks at the end and conclusion of the party, were the most significant aspects of a great event that brought jubilation, exultation, and joy in the heart of every inhabitant. But the solemnity of the festivity reached its highest peak when the crowd of the faithful accompanied the statue of St. Anthony in procession with songs and chants.

On the eve of the festivity, the Saint was carried in procession from the homonymous church to the Mother Church. In the evening of the thirteenth day the longest procession began, passing through different streets of the town to bring St. Anthony back to his church.

The population accompanied the Saint the entire time, carried on their shoulders by 24 alternating men. Before joining the procession, many families would wait for the arrival of the Saint from a balcony illuminated by bright lamps. As he passed by, they would kneel down and pour a tray of flower petals and wheat on the statue as a sign of devotional offerings. When the offer arrived, the men who carried the saint would shout "Viva S. Antonio di Padova! Viva!" (Long live St. Anthony of Padua!) with all the ardor of a boundless faith.

The moving gestures of the devotees who approached the Saint with a deferential, submissive, reverent attitude at each of the stops, hanging offers on his vestments in banknotes, the crowd of barefoot men and women carrying long lit candles, who moved with difficulty in the cobbled streets, immersed in a state of complete abstraction from the things that surrounded them, the songs exalting the figure of the Patron Protector which broke the silence in chorus and radiated notes of mystery in the air, which like beams of light touched the sensitivity of all the faithful, were the most exhilarating aspects and connotations of the solemnity and sacredness with which the Poggiorealese loved to celebrate this holiday. Saint Anthony was and still is the comfort of our villagers in every moment of anguish, pain, despair, and discouragement. And our fellow citizens have brought this devotion with them, wherever they emigrated in search of luck. The Poggiorealase community of Sydney, Australia deserves mention here, which celebrates and solemnizes the festivity with the same intensity and deep devotion as in the past.

The state of discomfort of those who leave their land, especially in the early days, is very often distressing. In a time not so long ago, they would set off with the hope of making their fortune, but also with the uncertainty of returning in more or less time. The detachment from the family of belonging at the moment of departure was heartbreaking; families cried for their relatives as if they were losing them forever; this painful scene remained indelible in the minds of the emigrants. The discomfort of finding oneself in a completely different environment, unaccustomed to their habits, the difficulties of communicating, living in a state of marginalization, the stressful lack of one's family, friends, things so dear and that belonged to their world so far away, in their lives, the memory of the streets where they spent their childhood, all the places they were connected to with strong emotions, sometimes emerged in their minds with exasperated nostalgia to the point of regretting ever having decided to leave. The moral and psychological discomfort prompted emigrants to cling to the spiritual comfort that could be given by faith and devotion to St. Anthony of Padua, instilled in their souls by their parents and ancestors.

The prayers to the Patron Saint of Poggioreale so that they could overcome social and moral discomfort and have the strength to fight and resist the sufferings of the heart, whose palpitations always flew to that small village scattered among the mountains in the distant land of Sicily, fueled their hopes of returning and finding fortune, and their relief from the daily malaise rested in this hope. And as the community of the Poggiorealese expanded and as their relationships intensified, a feeling of mutual solidarity grew more than it ever had when they were still in the same town of their origins, bringing our Poggiorealese of Sydney the desire to express the gratitude of the comfort that they rediscovered in the deepest faith in St. Anthony, celebrating the holiday with a solemn festivity in the distant land of Australia. So a committee was set up, led by a Chairman, with the aim of organizing the festivities in honor of the Saint every year, giving impetus and prestige to the celebration itself.

The festivity not only offers an opportunity for all the villagers to meet like a large family, but also brings the customs of an ancient tradition to mind, always at the heart of every Poggiorealese wherever he is, bringing back unforgettable memories of images and habits of a time that was always dear and alive, and renewing the nostalgia of the place of one's origins with deep emotion and inner turmoil.

As for the other religious festivals that were celebrated in the town, readers should refer to *Storia di Poggioreale* (History of Poggioreale) by Can. Dr. F.

Aloisio, who as a priest discusses their aspects and meanings with competence and analytical details.

However, it is important to recall the celebration of *San Giovanni, festa del solstizio d'estate* (St. John, festivity of the summer solstice), meaning the beginning of the season which by now goes unnoticed in our town where certain rites are no longer repeated, which in a not-so-distant past were still customary. I want to allude, for example, to the use of establishing the *comparatico* bond in the name of St. John, a spiritual union that had a greater value than a blood bond. The rite was articulated as follows: two boys or girls of close friendship decided to carry out the *comparatico* to strengthen their bond of friendship and make it lasting; on the day of St. John, June 24th, one of the two sent the other a basket full of seasonal fruit (pears, figs, *puma cannameli* (local apples)), sweets and some symbolic clothing; the other exchanged it for another basket filled in the same manner on St. Peter's day or on the same day. From that moment they had a companion or comrade for life. Another ritual practiced was to cut off a piece of each other's hair and exchange it, and from that moment on they became companions of *piliddu*.

Another festivity that is recalled with pleasure and is still observed is that of St. Lucia. In Poggioreale and Sicily and in many other regions, the worship of the Saint is linked to her role as protector of sight. This role was due to the literal interpretation of her name and to legend, according to which she tears out her eyes and sends them in a basin to her suitor, so he would give her up. It was customary, and is still handed down, to respect the holiday by avoiding eating bread on the day and eating only *cuccia*, that is, wheat cooked and then seasoned with cooked wine, today instead cooked with various creams and honey. Eating *cuccia* seasoned with cooked wine was the delight of all the children, and above all it represented a novelty that gave them so much joy and pleasure .

XXIII - FOLKLORE AND LIFE CYCLE

Other folklore traditions have accompanied man in the stages of life, such as birth, engagement, weddings, etc. These customs and beliefs are called rites of passage because they indicate that set of ceremonies that take place in the succession of these different periods of a person's life. For example, the customs relating to marriage capture the various passages ranging from the declaration of the young man's love to the girl's acceptance to the other rituals that characterize the wedding, the entrance of the bride into the new home, the first wedding night and so on. In short, there are rules to be followed and taboos to be respected, so that the forces of good prevail and those of evil are kept at bay.

The rituals have ancient origins, we will say pagan, which were then corrected by Christianity, which in its 20 centuries of existence has fought against superstitious manifestations contrary to morality and religion.

Taking the above into account, many customs and beliefs of the Poggiorealese population had a common root with those of other Italian and foreign regions. In our town, for example, sterility was seen as misfortune; apart from the fact that considering it as such is still a spontaneous and natural reaction of couples, in an era in which fertility was welcomed as a grace of the Lord and children were Providence, sterility was even seen as a divine curse. Hence the use of certain propitiatory rites, to which even the sterile women of our town were subjected in the strictest confidentiality. It is known that in some regions of Italy, before sleeping with their husbands, sterile brides would wear the shirt of a woman who had had many children, or would touch another mother, because they believed in prolific virtue acquired through contact.

Among the families of our ancestors, St. Anne was invoked so that the new couple would be granted the gift of children. Today this belief still exists, but is not directed towards fighting sterility; St. Anne is invoked for trouble-free childbirth.

Voluntary sterility was totally opposed then and condemned by public opinion; in fact, the families of our grandparents were quite numerous. And the condemnation of voluntary sterility was widespread not only in Sicily, but also in other European regions. In Great Britain it was even believed that a woman guilty of such a sin would be reincarnated as a sow with many piglets.

Returning to the confines of Poggioreale, certain beliefs which are still widespread deserve mention, although their legacy is beginning to fade, in relation to the cravings of pregnant women: she must not scratch or touch any part of herself while she is craving something, in order to prevent the baby from being born with a birthmark in the point where she had scratched. Another belief that continues today is that you must never refuse a pregnant woman anything she is craving, as the child will have birthmarks on their skin and other deformities that are interpreted as cravings for strawberries, coffee, grapes, etc.

Another widespread practice was the criterion of predicting the sex of the unborn child through the physiological observation of the belly: if the woman had a pointed belly, a male would be born, if rounded a female.

Sometimes the predictions were based on the lunar months and astronomical calculations: if the moon was waxing, it was a male, if the moon was waning a female. Or still the experiment with a wishbone from a chicken: it was thrown on the table, and if it fell with the fork up, it would have been a female, otherwise a male.

The birth of a male was met with joy and was undoubtedly more welcome than a girl. The reasons for this preference were based firstly on the pride of the father, who saw the perpetuation of the family name in his son, and also because other strong young arms would collaborate with the father in the hard work of the countryside within a few decades, with the consequent improvement of the entire family's living conditions. The traditions relating to childbirth reflected some typical practices of a certain level of hygienic-sanitary cognition. In more remote times, the *mammana* was an experienced woman, then in more recent times a licensed midwife was given the same name *mammana*. After being bathed, the newborn was wrapped up tight like a mummy and perhaps a few amulets were hidden in the folds, because it was believed that the new mother and newborn were subject to the action of evil spirits and thus various means of protection were used. For example, a light was kept on even at night, suggested by a practical precaution to keep the newborn monitored at night and quickly intervene in case of any regurgitation that could suffocate it; well, this caution was interpreted as a defense of the newborn from the intervention of the evil one, facilitated by the darkness of night. The cradle was also considered a dwelling subject to all the forces of evil, and thus protective magical means, such as a red bow, were used as protection.

The cradle of the newborn was called "*naca*", which comes from *naxe,* meaning sheepskin fleece, as they were once made of this material. The modest peasant families usually had cradles shaped in an archaic, simple way: two ropes fixed on the sides of a corner of the house, a blanket settled between the two ropes to form a sort of hanging bed, whose swinging accompanied by the singsong of a lullaby would send the baby off to sleep.

The child entered the social circle of Christians with Baptism. The date of this religious liturgy, in the period when popular tradition was most practiced, was set as soon as possible in consideration of the frequent infantile illnesses due to the lack of medical care and the modest hygienic and dietary conditions. In fact, it is said that immediately after the sacred rite, the godmother gave the child back to the new mother pronouncing the sacramental phrase: "You gave him to me pagan and I give him back to you Christian."

In popular tradition, the godparents at the baptism assume a position of very close spiritual kinship equal to that of blood in the newborn's family. In certain places, it was the godfather who gave the newborn his name. In Poggioreale, as in many other Italian and foreign regions, the name was given according to an ancient tradition that is still valid in many families: first the names of the paternal grandparents are given, then the maternal ones and then those of the uncles. At the end of the baptism ceremony, the family returns to the baby's house followed by the procession of relatives and friends, as well as the group of boys and girls who had run to the church following the sound of the bells announcing the ceremony. Once home, the ceremony consisted of offering pink or blue sugared almonds to guests depending on the sex of the newborn, roasted chickpeas and fava beans and some alcoholic beverages: liqueur or wine.

In the very first months, the mother was responsible for the baby's growth and education, with the frequent collaboration of the grandmother or other spinster aunts always on the maternal side, when there were many children and they had been born at intervals close to each other. When a couple established their home, according to a very widespread mentality in the town, the bride continued to maintain relationships with her family of origin with a pestering frequency, it was said daily, while she limited herself to visiting her in-laws on Sundays and not necessarily regularly. The girls approached their weddings with prejudices about them instilled in the girls by their families, perhaps out of jealousy and fear that once their daughter's hand was given away in matrimony, she would share her affection for her parents with the husband's parents as well. The wife's attachment to her family of origin involved her husband as well, with the result that he visited his bride's relatives much more and neglected his parents. Hence the motto: "*Li parenti di la mughieri su duci corno lù mèli, chiddi di lù maritu su gairi comu l'acitu.*" (The wife's relatives are as sweet as honey, the husband's relatives are as sour as vinegar.)

Therefore, the relatives of the maternal family had a successful educational impact, whose connotation reflected distinctive and typical customs, traditions, culture, habits, and mentalities of the environment of belonging. In general, games, rules, forms, and ideas were put into practice that were important from the pedagogical, ethnographic, and demographic point of view, within a pedagogy based on the experience of many generations. Simply consider the riddles, tongue twisters for sharpening one's wits, stories, fairy tales, and writing boards for developing the use of the imagination, prayers for instilling religious sentiment, and lastly the different games that children played to develop dexterity, skill, intelligence, ingenuity.

Many games of the Poggiorealese youth reflected the uses, rituals, and beliefs once practiced by mature men. For example, when children sing and run in a circle, they are reproducing a ceremony requesting one's hand typical of nuptial practices in the Middle Ages. The game of "cops and robbers" can be said to have attracted the most aristocratic Italian society to the fields outside the city almost until the end of the 18th century; it was the same in France according to L. Becques de Fouquieres[1] and S. La Sorsa[2]; the game "blind man's bluff" was thoroughly enjoyed by our children, while in the Middle Ages it was a common party game. The trick of bouncing pebbles on the surface of water was practiced by the ancient Greeks and was called "epostrachismos" (see the discussion *Octavius* by the Christian writer Minucio Felice); according to information handed down to us by Plato, Aristophanes, Pliny, Virgil and Ovid, the Greeks and the Romans enjoyed playing with a spinning top, which has long disappeared in our environment today; playing with balls was just as ancient and universally widespread: Homer mentions it when writing about Ulysses' landing on the island of the Phaeacians. Lastly, we must recall the game of buttons that was so widespread among the children of the peasant families, called "*cozzo patate*" and "*travu longu*". It is thus clear that games have an ancient history and sometimes a meaning which is much more interesting than what is usually attributed to them.

The lightheartedness of the age for playing games of our ancestors was interrupted by the assignment of responsibilities far above their age: often at seven/eight years old, a child's parents would entrust them with a task that extinguished the lightheartedness of a soul that, although still open to welcome the dreams of imagination, must face the disappointing reality of life. In addition to Communion and Confirmation, which marked rites of passage from one age to another, the most important stages in the lives of young people were, and still are, engagement and marriage. The customs that led a young man from celibacy to marriage were generally shared by other small rural towns in western Sicily.

1 *Les jeux des anciens,* L. Baques de Fouquieres, Paris.
2 *Come giocano i fanciulli d'Italia* (How children play in Italy), S. La Sorsa.

-123-

As mentioned, as a small, rural, popular town, Poggioreale was closed to cultural influences due to its state of isolation and the lack of means and paths of communication, as well as the state of illiteracy and semi-literacy of the population. The patrimony of local culture consisted in all those rules, sayings, proverbs, customs which when put together, represented the source of the education of a village mentality, inclined to the rigorous respect of social and moral values, as well as conventions, whose transgression compromised the dignity and esteem of the person before all. From this state of closure, it follows that two spouses were usually chosen within their village circle, that is, the tradition of endogamy dominated, confirmed by the widespread proverb that reads: "*Moglie e buoi dei paesi tuoi*" (Wife and oxen from your town).

Considering then that the young woman had to maintain a chaste, reserved attitude in terms of customs, moderation, and simplicity both in clothing and in behavior, that she did not have the possibility, nor the freedom to take a walk along the main road of the town with other friends of the same age, that occasional outings with her mother and other older relatives were rare, the possibilities of encounters, meetings, the forms of courtship between the young men and women were limited to very few occasions: vigils, the intense agricultural work, the religious and non-religious holidays, Sunday mass, and the fountain where she would go to draw water. Sunday Mass was the most frequent occasion: it gave the girls the opportunity to wear their nicest dress and fix their hair as best they could to make themselves attractive to the people, but above all to lure a young suitor, who free from work, would punctually attend church and stick his head around the colonnade of the aisles, peeking among the rows of chairs reserved for the women in search of a girl to focus on. At the end of mass, the men then lined up in the open space in front of the church door and reviewed the girls who would pass by upon exiting, some more embarrassed and quite shy, while others much more flirtatious and forward. In this case, the encounters between the young men and women were left to a spontaneous natural fondness, but many other opportunities for encounters were arranged by families who focused their intentions more on economic convenience than on feelings of love, uttering "*il letto fa l'affetto*" (the bed makes affection). So it was not only the figure of the young woman, whether she was beautiful or ugly, if she could be a good housewife and a clean and submissive wife, as well as a caring mother of a family, but also her dowry, meaning if she would come with a house (which was customary as a dowry, while the expenses for the furniture and furnishings were borne by the groom's family), a good dowry of linen. This latter fact was so important that days before the wedding, the linen was laid out before friends and relatives and was a source of pride of the bride's family, seeking compliments for a rich, valuable dowry: sheets finely embroidered by the same bride, tablecloths, nightgowns that embellished the bride's body in the eyes of the groom, soliciting his urges of desire and love, and many other items designed to meet the daily needs of the bride and the couple. The mother of the family began to prepare the linen for her daughters from the time they were little; in fact, a saying went: *"figlia in fasce, biancheria 'nti la cascia"* (daughter swaddled up, linen in the trunk).

If then there was also a *salma* of land to enrich the dowry, the young lady's marriage requests multiplied, and she also had the privilege of choosing between the farmer or the "master," between a more seductive young man and another less seductive one; these were all the privileges that at times helped a less attractive girl find a husband, while those who had nothing had to hope they were very beautiful and attractive, otherwise there was the risk of remaining a spinster.

The engagement became official when the parents, generally the mother of the young man, asked the girl's family for their daughter's hand. If the girl's parents, who were the interpreters of their daughter's will, accepted the request, the next step was the "recognition," during which the two young people and their families met; if the young woman rejected the suitor, the messenger would return home with his arms hanging down and his face mortified, keeping the *coffa* (the rejection) in the strictest confidentiality. A young girl's refusal was shameful for the young man. The expression - asking for the hand in marriage - derives from the ancient use of *toccamano,* (meaning touch hands), which is the ancient "dextrarum conjunctio" that was carried out between the engaged to sanction the mutual promise of marriage.

At the moment of the request and acceptance it was customary, at least until the beginning of the 20th century, to draw up the list of the girl's dowry and linens. Always according to tradition, the "recognition" was followed soon after by a ceremony called the "*accordamento*" (agreement), an occasion in which the engagement ring was usually offered as a gift; this was the official gift of "entry" of the young man's family into the house of the promised bride. From that moment on and for the entire period of the engagement, the relationships between the two families were regulated by customs and ceremonies of mutual respect, which demonstrated the importance of the new alliance between families: the exchange of gifts and enjoying meals together during the most significant holidays. The *accordamento* ceremony included invitations to friends and relatives, who were offered green sugared almonds, the color of hope, along with homemade sweets, liqueur, wine and other delicacies.

The young man would visit his promised bride's house during all his free time and like a fly on honey, would take advantage of any moments in which he could evade the rigorous surveillance of her mother to steal a few drops of nectar from the young woman. Before their engagement, the young Poggiorealese men usually passed their time with other men: there were no outings with both boys and girls as happens today; there were no lively and close friendships between young boys and girls such as to create a relationship of innocent familiarity between them. The young boys were always pleased to talk about women conquered or to be conquered with their friends, about extraordinary adventures, fleeting meetings, perhaps all conquests of fantasy, told with swagger to highlight their own entrepreneurship in the difficult approaches with the girls to the others. In fact, a simple smile from the girl was enough, immediately interpreted as a sign of malicious provocation. If a boy and a girl found themselves facing each other, they behaved not as if they were man and woman, but simply male and female. They could entertain friendship, but any sudden sparks could cause a short circuit. Hence the woman's defensive attitude. She had a tendency to shyness: from childhood she lived in a climate of obsession with sin and therefore did everything she could to be aware of it. But when she passed over the circle of fire imposed by morality, then she knew how to recognize the forbidden taste of excesses.

The gift of the ring as a symbol of *'ngaggiamento*, or rather of the "agreement," dates back to distant times and is still in use in some families; while in even more remote times, most likely the bond between the two young people was symbolized in rural towns by the *nzinga*, a ribbon with which the future mother-in-law tied the hair of the future daughter-in-law.

After the engagement ceremonies, the next step was the preparations for the wedding. The choice of the wedding date was very important. For example, no weddings are held in the month of May; this tradition dates back to Roman times, who considered the month of May ominous for weddings. The use then continued in the Christian world, justified by a different reason: May is the month dedicated to the Virgin, hence the proverb: "*la sposa maialina non si gode la cuttunìna*" (the May bride does not enjoy a warm blanket).

The choice of the date was also related to different social and economic conditions, as well as seasonal work. As for the days of the week, Saturday or Sunday was preferred and Friday was bad luck and was usually excluded.

The bath of the bride and groom on the eve of the wedding was a preliminary ritual. In the morning the bride's clothing was particularly important. Up until the 1920s, the bride's wedding dress was not usually white, but a soft and unlively color, preferably light pink, unlike the bright colors that

Photo 31 - Newlyweds accompanied in procession
-127-

were used in other regions of Southern Italy and other European countries. The use of a white dress in popular environments is related to more recent times, perhaps due to the influence exerted by the dogma of the Immaculate Conception. Over time, the wedding wreath made of orange blossoms or roses has joined the veil in imitation of the virgin in her marriage with Joseph, a symbol of virginity.

Originally the color of flames *(flammeum)* in the wedding rites of the Romans with the symbolic meaning of innocence, the veil was an innovation with respect to more remote eras and, as we know, in the wedding of the rich and noble it was very long and held up by children or pages. Today it has become smaller and in the most evolved areas it tends to disappear. According to some scholars of Sicilian folklore, the veil came to replace the cloak. The Pitrè Museum has several specimens, including a black cloak that Sciacca's bride wore in the 18th century to reach the altar. Similarly, the exchange of wedding rings, placed on the ring finger upon the consecration of the marriage in church *(le cinturette)* as a symbol of fidelity and bonding, represents a phase of the development and tangible evolution of the use of the belt around the bride's hips as she walked to the altar. But the tangible representation also expands with all the jewels in the shape of a circle: necklaces, rings and so on. Hence the use of the *cinturetta* to be worn on the ring finger, because in the Middle Ages it was believed that it corresponded to a vein of the heart. The use of the belt was very ancient and formed an indispensable element in the clothing of Greek and Roman brides, but its origin perhaps dates back to certain customs of the primitive populations such as the Vedda of Ceylon, where matrimony was confirmed when the man and woman tied a reed cord at their sides.

On the morning of the wedding, before leaving for the ceremony in the church, the bride would wait for the groom to arrive. Once he arrived with his relatives and guests, the procession to walk to the church was formed. It was customary for the bride to walk with her hand in her father's, while the groom gave his hand to his mother. After the ceremony, the procession was led by the bride and groom (see photo no. 31).

During the passage of the bride and groom, sugar-coated almonds, wheat, and coins were thrown at them to wish them fertility and prosperity. In some towns firecrackers were set off as a sign of celebration, even if in ancient times they were intended to ward off evil spirits.

The wedding ceremonies ended with the reception of friends and relatives, who were offered sweets and glasses of liqueur of various colors prepared by the families of the newlyweds, with lunch reserved for the closest relatives and finally in the evening, accompanying the couple in procession to their new home. In truth, the wedding ceremony did not end there because in

Poggioreale, as in many other Sicilian towns, there was also the custom that in the morning the mother of the bride would go their house to help the bride and groom "rise well," bringing coffee or pigeon broth especially intended for the groom; certainly, on that occasion she had to treat him well, always for the love of her daughter. And it is fortunate that the task of showing the groom's parents the proof of the virginity preserved by the young woman until marriage had fallen into disuse. As has the custom of staying in the house for eight days doing nothing but making love has also disappeared. Perhaps this custom was explained in the principle of not creating any sort of distractions or impediments to the pleasures of love. After the eight days the bride and groom would go to Mass and finally make their appearance among the people.

A new family unit had been formed and integrated into the social community of Poggiorealese life, where the women's role in the peasant town, as has been said about the family, assumed important social responsibilities. The men left the village at dawn for work that lasted from dawn to dusk and often from Monday to Saturday or perhaps even beyond, and the women, the children and the elderly stayed within the confined spaces of the town, among the alleys and the courtyards. And it was the women who had relations with the neighborhood, who managed and interpreted family interests, who set the behavioral rules that were very binding for the entire community. The codes of the urban aggregate were consolidated, managed, filtered by female decisions, which were then accepted by the men. Thus the new bride prepared to become "this central character in the economy of the peasant family, exalting the stability of its aggregating function"[1].

The poet Mario Gori realistically grasped the characteristics of the family in rural environments and the life that takes place there. His poem *Sud* reads: "The south has mud roads/ and hedges of agave and brambles / and low houses tinted with smoke / and women dressed in black / who wash in front of the doors / and wait for men and mules / with anxious eyes, dark and gloomy. And men have the south / dressed in military coats / and maffiosi caps, / their bones tired from years of hoeing / and the dark blood of silence and love. / The South prays and blasphemes / the black saints of the processions. / And old men still have my south,/ beggars of sunshine, / old men who drink wine / and weave threads of reed / and patch nets / and tell of old misfortunes. / He throws oil on water/ for girls who have walnut breasts / and wait for the bites of men / and on the water then salt / spitting saracen words / against evil eyes and spells. / But you get lost in the south at twenty for a red carnation." M. Gori's poem fully grasps the life of hardships and unspeakable efforts of the farmer and

[1]Giuseppe Giarrizzo, *Civiltà contadina* (Peasant civilization), Bari, 1980.

above all a significant opposition: on the one hand the women dressed in black, painful Penelopi, who await husbands returning from the fields every Saturday night, on the other the girls greedy for love, even before their wedding rites. The result is an inner division between duty and transgression in an atmosphere of trepidation.

Even the death that closes the cycle of human life was accompanied by rites and customs that were once customary in our town (which have now partially disappeared) and common to almost all the other small agricultural towns of Southern Italy. First of all, it is appropriate to begin with the fact that the disappearance of a person is learned by the people of the town with almost all the townspeople sharing in the sadness. The town belonged to those who lived there, unlike the city and the metropolises, which belong not only to those who live there, but also to those who arrive and those who leave. Anonymity is the dominant connotation between traffic and the hastily moving crowd, all caught up in the day's commitments without looking anyone in the face and without possibly having the comfort of at least a greeting. In towns, we all know each other, and human and social contact takes place without scheduling meetings and appointments, without prearranging the instinctive need of man to socialize, to exchange opinions, to feel like an integral part of the community of one's environment in good and bad. The festivities, anniversaries, weddings, births, deaths and all the events of the daily life of a population are characterized by the participation of all the inhabitants. Any event passes from one mouth to another and becomes public knowledge, followed by comments, gossip, the expression of negative or positive opinions; everything that happens within a family takes place in more extended and less affected forms. In fact, the inhabitants of a small urban town live like a large family with the manifestations of affection or hatred, solidarity, understanding and deception, hypocrisy, impulses of love and anger; but very often when faced with disaster or death, there is solidarity and grief.

When the sad, lamenting sound of the bells announcing the death of someone was heard by the people, it was followed by a startle that stopped all the actions of the mind and body for a moment to give way to the impulses of the heart that transmits a note of languor and sadness to the whole body; at first there is an awareness of the precariousness of human life, which goes out to reach those who know the other shores; immediately after comes the image of a lifeless body, rigid, insensitive to the anguish of the family members who will lose them forever. Then curiosity prompted to ask neighbors for information: assumptions were made about people whose illness was known to be more or less serious and finally the certainty came, accompanied by the expression of solidarity with the family members and of consternation: "*mischinu, che bravu omu! ancora giuvani si nni iu e lassau la famigghia 'mmèzzu la strata,*" (What a shame, he was such a good man! so young to leave his family in misery now) or "*chi dispiaciri ! era anzianu, ma un omu bonu,*" (I'm so sorry! He was old but he was a good man). And the neighbor commenting on what happened with the other neighbor next door would say: "*bedda matri, stamattina mi sdivigghiài cu lu cori 'ncuttumatu, 'ntisi una miula cantari stanotte*" (Mother of God, this morning I woke up with an anguished heart, I heard an owl hooting last night) (the call of the owl, the call of the hen that crows like a rooster, or the howling of a dog in the silence of the night were considered bad omens).

Among the most common customs in the case of death, in addition to that of opening the door of the compartment intended for the coffin, was covering mirrors with black veils, as well as fixing a black strap behind the front door of the house with the words: "for my husband, for my father," etc.

The manifestation of pain was not only a personal expression of the internal torment of the relatives, but also a ritual demonstrating their pain that was fulfilled with cries of distress, tearing at their hair, and with the funeral song, called *repitio* or *ripitàri*. This funeral song recalled Homer's *Iliad* and the Greek tragedy where the closest relatives sang, such as his wife, mother, sister or by women who lent themselves for compensation, the precious women also called "*reputatrici*" (women who were paid to loudly sing and lament during funerals). Another custom was the funeral lunch, called *consùlu*. The relatives or friends awaited the return of their relatives from the cemetery, because as grieved as they were, they could not take care of any sort of practical matters.

The traditional customs related to death were prolonged with the mourning that was a proof of the continuity of the affective relations between the dead and those still alive. During the strong mourning period the men let their beards grow and wore a black cap and black band on their arms; this period lasted up to two years. Black would become the standard color for the woman, since the mourning lasted so long that by the time she was ready to stop wearing black, another death requiring black would occur. Today many of these manifestations of pain and mourning are almost gone; the pain is certainly there, but it is contained to avoid harrowing scenes or funeral songs. Black is beginning to be worn less and less by the younger generations, and the older ones complain about the lack of respect for those who have passed.

XXIV - POGGIOREALE FROM THE POST-WAR PERIOD TO THE 1968 EARTHQUAKE

On September 8, 1943, the Badoglio government ended the armistice with the Anglo-Americans. For a moment the Italians deluded themselves that the war was over; instead, the war continued in our area: the center-north was invaded by the Germans and the Anglo-Americans were advancing from the South. The civil struggle between the Italians of the Resistance, who had formed the National Liberation Committees, and the remnants of fascism represented by the puppet government of the Republic of Salò, were also fought in the middle of the war.

The armistice that was supposed to save Italy generated a phenomenon of dissolution. In a few hours Italy found itself without a government, without administration and without an army. The king and the marshal had secretly fled Rome without even warning the ministers, without giving instructions to the generals who commanded the six divisions that were to ensure the defense of Rome. The State was no more.

Among the generals, the prefects, the directors-general, and the quaestors, some abandoned their offices, others lacked the initiative of those who are accustomed to acting within a climate of freedom, as they were accustomed to serving only one master. Now that the master was no longer there, they were frightened and lost, without guidance. In such circumstances there was no need for orders from above, for the administration to continue to function, and for the departments of the armed forces to maintain discipline, the real problem was that they did not have sufficient training that would allow them to take the necessary initiatives on the path to follow.

And so a few days later, that is, on September 8th, little remained of the army, divisions, and regiments. Soldiers and officers found themselves surrounded by problems and left to fend for themselves with the only goal of reaching their city or town. They had to take refuge among woods and paths, after having put on civilian clothes provided, upon request, by peasant families they met on the street. Many of these disbanded men faced various dangers, regardless of whether they came from the North to reach the South or vice versa. They avoided the carriageways, travelling many miles on foot and helping themselves with makeshift equipment along secondary roads and always afraid of an unfortunate encounter with German patrols.

From September 8, 1943 to April 25, 1945, the date of the liberation of the entire country and the creation of the first government of free Italy (the Parri government), the lack of the State in the entire national territory was felt, albeit with gradual and slow processes of recovery of established order.

The reflections of these inconveniences were therefore also found in Poggioreale. When the threat of the law is weakened by the catastrophic results of a war that brings a country to its knees, paralyzing its resources and creating forms of social, political, moral, and economic disarray, men more prone to evil take advantage of it and unleash the most degenerate instincts. The Machiavellian concept of State is based precisely on the pessimistic vision that the author has of man: he cannot contain his selfish instinct, making order impossible within an established society; therefore, the fear of the State and its laws is necessary. Thus the State everything and any measure aimed at safeguarding life becomes permitted for the good of society.

Poggioreale suffered the consequences of this state of affairs by living periods of uncertainty and insecurity.

And it is fortunate that it did not bear witness to the deadly clashes of the belligerent armies, nor the bombings that reduced many cities to ruins, nor the retaliations of the Germans, of which many innocent people and children had been victims, nor the deportation to the concentration camps in Germany, nor lastly the psychosis of fear, when the air was suddenly torn by the deafening sound of sirens. That sound penetrated the bodies of the people pushing them to run, like so many madmen towards the shelters among the shouts of fear and terror.

But the war also touched our town. How many mothers experienced moments of anguish and hope for their children! The young sons scattered on different fronts and of which there was no news! What sorrow for the families who fought for news of their children missing in Russia or killed on the battlefield or deported as prisoners in Germany! And so many expectations were disappointed, the expectations of those young Poggiorealese who fell in the war, breaking the lives of all the mothers who clung to a very thin thread of hope until the last moment. Now a monument reminds of the sacrifice of their lives, but it also serves as a warning that we must fight for peace in the world with all the strength of ideas and actions capable of inspiring feelings of solidarity in a world in which the people, thanks to the amazing means of information and communication, could find, with the gradualness required by the times, the ways to solve the serious problems that beset all of humanity.

There were all kinds of difficulties; there were acts of vandalism towards state structures and everything that was part of the public administration. Merely to cite an example, the farmhouses that had been built during the fascist period were attacked, and the doors, windows, roof tiles, and even the pieces of tuff of the perimeter walls were taken away. We remember the raids of the ammunition depots abandoned by the military in disarray; the savage looting of the military subsistence services depots when the German departments that had custody of them received the order to abandon everything and leave immediately.

Criminal acts became frequent, continuous robbery and theft were complained of; small gangs of thugs formed that made the life of the local population insecure.

War is catastrophe, it is death and suffering, it is the destruction of everything that a population has built through years of hard work and sweat, but it is also a jolt out of the state of tolerance to the habits of daily life, an awakening of the mind numbed by the secular condition of closure which had paralyzed the initiatives and impetus towards new goals in the quality of life.

The terror of war, the states of anxiety, the dangers to which a person is subjected from one moment to the next disturb the conscience, generate states of anguish, and by reaction release forms of attachment to life, with all the ardor of an inner force never felt in daily life before. In times of danger, people appreciate the values of life, take a step back and realize the drowsiness that has characterized their existence, hence the intentions aimed at improving its conditions and living it more intensely, always within the limits of those slow and gradual developments allowed by the work resources, environmental conditions, and spaces in which it is possible to act. And the need to activate evolutionary developments in living conditions not only arises as a result of a psychological fact promoted by the state of belligerence of a people, but also from the occasional opportunity that the young people, called to arms, had to broaden the horizons of the mind and internalize new cultural contacts and new experiences, even if these were matured in the climate of dramatic human disaster that was war. This is not intended to justify war as an event that, although catastrophic, is a harbinger of the renewal of peoples, pushing them to awaken from their habitual slumber and to accelerate the steps towards more advanced development goals. My reflection is not an extraction of Marinetti's futurism that has no qualms exalting war as a moment of destruction and futuristic impulses. If so, I would be in contradiction with myself or it would be as if in Leopardi's poem, *La quiete dopo la tempesta* (The Calm After the Storm), one wanted to give the interpretation that the poet justifies the advent of the storm, so that the people, in the moment when the quiet returns, reap happiness for the danger they have evaded.

So a new mentality began to mature in the conscience of the young people who, while continuing to live in a still semi-feudal structure with attitudes of a social role subordinate compared to the "civil," disdained the slavish submission to their fathers and the reverent "kiss of the hands" with bowing and removing their hats. This phenomenon had its roots in the distant 1920s with symptoms of imperceptible development since the small autonomous farms begin to spread following the division of the lands (1927).

The spread of the radio in the early fifties in the least deprived families, the establishment of lines of connection with Palermo, Trapani, Alcamo, Castelvetrano, and other towns with comfortable buses favored the rupture of the centuries-old isolation, in whose borders the roots of the entire set of customs, beliefs and fears that had been ravaged by time were increasingly deep.

The contraband of wheat, favored by membership (*tesseramento*), led to a considerable increase in the price of wheat - it had reached the paradoxical figure of about 42,000 lire per *salma* (about 500 lb.) -, had favored the economy of many families who risked severe penalties, even if rising above a state of atavistic misery.

Even the solicitations of the members of the left parties that formed immediately after the end of the war contributed to laying the foundations for a social emancipation of the entire category of the *borgesato*, the small settlers and the laborers. It is true that the membership of the socialist and communist party consisted of the working class, small settlers, and poor people who lived on hardships and occasional arrangements, but it is also true that the rallies of the socialist exponents shook the sensibilities of some marginal fringes of sharecroppers and *gabelloti* and urged a faded memory of ancient resentments that had been hidden and become resignation. Yet they listened to the rallies at a distance so as not to affect the relationships of convenience and dependence with the owners of the land they had been entrusted with. Then there was also a broad range of small independent owners in the town who were pleased to feel like part of the middle *borghese* class, very close to the upper middle class and to accept the Don in the likeness of the hegemonic caste. The members of this social class were careful not to mingle with the lesser people, first because of a question of class distinction and then because they feared that that small and modest property they had earned with enormous sacrifices and savings would run the risk of ending up in the hands of the communists and socialists.

It is also important to consider the fear of the families, especially the women, that the advance of communism would force the denial of God and suppress the freedom of worship.

To tell the truth, until the early 1950s the town's economy, as indeed in the whole of Southern Italy, was still backward and primitive: it was a generally poor agricultural economy at a very low technological level, scarcely mobile, therefore basically static without resources. The houses were still without running water and hygienic services, but there was an unmatured predisposition to travel less-constraining paths that led towards different life perspectives than that of their fathers.

This openness was not a consciously desired fact due to determinations made from today to tomorrow, but a social phenomenon that began to ferment very slowly and in relation to the natural evolution of the changing times and for the prudence of the farmers who loved tranquility; they worked in the countryside, they saw to the needs of their farm, avoiding the harassment of people who were sometimes pleased to disturb others, to satisfy an inclination to evil.

At this point, I think the moment has come to make some historical reference to the mafia phenomenon in Sicily.

We already know that since the medieval ages up to the beginning of the 20th century, the feudal lords imposed their laws of malfeasance on their subjects and their families. Those who declared themselves unwilling to suffer this state of subjugation had no alternative but to take to the woods, enlarging the numerous ranks of bandits who infested the countryside. Many bandits stole from the rich and gave to the poor to relieve them of their suffering.

To eliminate these outlaws, in 1770 the feudal lords formed so-called companies of arms of ex-convicts to combat the phenomenon of banditry. So it happened that the people of Sicily had to suffer, in addition to the hegemonic attitude of the rich, also the misdeeds of these criminals who divided the island territory into areas of influence, in which it seemed that order reigned, but it was the order of their impositions and not that of justice. In fact, he who had been robbed of mules and cattle was forced not to file a complaint and the robber to return what had been stolen for compensation. If the robbed party refused to accept this proposal, a forest, a ditch, the riverbed of a stream awaited him. This medieval legacy continued to exist until the unity of Italy and beyond, indeed, thanks to the political cover, it became more powerful for the services rendered to Giuseppe Garibaldi's Expedition of the Thousand and to the island politicians who sat on the benches of the Italian Parliament. Many

168

Photo 32 - Clothing styles of the late 1800s
-137

services were carried out by the mafia for the island farmers to impose their will on the peasants and laborers in relation to the agrarian contracts. The most eloquent example is represented by the bloody events of Gibellina, following the *Fasci dei lavoratori* revolt of 1893, which was, as we know, a mass popular organization that asked for the modification of the leasing and sharecropping agreements, because those in force were too onerous. The intransigence of the owners and the gentlemen unleashed an uproar that was then suffocated in the blood of the Sicilian Francesco Crispi.

With fascism, thanks to the presence of the prefect Cesare Mori equipped with special powers, the impression was given that the mafia had disappeared from Sicily and emigrated to America, but in reality the mafia had three tendencies: one of emigration to America, a second of servility towards the fascist state, from which it continued to profit legally, and a third of pausing its wrongdoings while waiting for better times.

Immediately after the Second World War, the mafia awoke from its apparent lethargy to resume its activities of association for delinquency and with more refined weapons, so much so as to penetrate the body of the State and the emerging Sicilian Region. The 1947 massacre of *Portella della Ginestra* of defenseless workers who were celebrating political and trade union freedoms on May 1st was an emblematic example of the resumption of mafia activity in the service of the large estates. With the advent of the 1950s, the mafia abandoned the feuds for the city, pushing public functions to moral and civil degradation, so much so that a political-mafia alliance was justified with the need to expand the front of the fight against Communism, as if it were a territorial control structure for electoral and administrative purposes.

The reappearance of the phenomenon with even more virulence following the fall of fascism proved harmful to the larger cities, rather than to a small municipality like Poggioreale where the tranquility of our population was disturbed more by small thefts, robberies, and greed at the hands of improvised thieves who took advantage of the state of the institutions' disbandment. However, the news of banditry that operated in other areas of our island, certain reminiscences of the times before fascism, intimately revealed the unfolding of the unconscious longing for a life freer from forms of subjection, no longer justified by a reality that, although moving among old patterns, revealed new purposes, and moved in different fields compared to the recent past. In fact, the presence of a student son in many *borgesi* families, the measures of the agrarian reform of the De Gasperi government which, although failing in the objective of reducing the large estates to 200 hectares of land, did however undermine a feudal system, the establishment of the *Cassa per il mezzogiorno* (Funds for the South) that issued credit measures in favor of farms and contributions for the purchase of equipment, accelerated the momentum of the Poggiorealese agricultural environment towards new relational approaches.

The old social and civil structure was replaced by new habits, new interests, new mental spaces that found confirmation in manifestations and behaviors of freer expression of personality.

The gradual spread of mechanization which had begun to take shape since the early fifties, the adoption of new working techniques favored by the use of mechanical means, and with the consequent increase in grain production the tendency to prefer intensive crops such as that of the vineyards, gave proof of a more advanced social entity. Above all, the large farms began to use tractors, harvesters, threshers that moved from one location to another, saving men from the heavy and bestial labors of the past. Yet many small farms proved more reluctant to innovate, at least in the early days, perhaps due to lack of adequate resources, also of an economic nature.

The styles of clothing also changed: the women no longer wore the old black cloaks, nor lace shawls, nor the ancient high-necked dresses (see photo no. 32) and the men began to stop wearing velvet suits designed for the holidays, and for work they no longer wore trousers with a thousand patches, nor used olona or waxed canvas *prantàli* (pants). The children were no longer called to work when still in school age; the migratory flow to Northern Italy, Switzerland, Germany, Australia, and the providential relief institutions for the labor force such as checks, wages, mutual funds all contributed to improving the town's economy.

The gradual replacement of gas at the old domestic hearth that tended to eliminate wood and coal for cooking, the tendency to buy bread at homemade or electric bakeries with the consequent and slow abandonment of the family ovens, the presence of equipped bars where people could enter for coffee, ice cream and other drinks, the various grocery stores, the numerous butcher shops that began to equip themselves with refrigerators, the meeting and game clubs, the electric oil mills, the passage of families and girls who during the weekends would enter and exit bars for ice cream without scandalizing anyone, the low-cut clothing of women no longer engaged in field work, the widespread use of makeup by young woman who began to beautify themselves and wear lipstick, an act which was entirely reprehensible and allowed only in women of theater in the past, all aspects characterizing the 1950s and 60s, are all testimony of

Photo 33 - Peasant's clothes
-140-

the breakdown of the peasant civilization, even if the new was not experienced in terms of opposition to the old, on the contrary it went hand in hand with the old and without disturbing contrasts.

Another historically significant testimony of the regression of the peasant town that wavered under the weight of a social and political structure (or impetus) inspired by the democratic comparison of ideas was given by the administrative elections of May 1956, when the electoral list of the left represented by a young teacher, Vincenzo Caronia, was victorious. Thanks to a broad popular following, he faced his competition of the outgoing Mayor on the right with determination. The rising of the guard of the young man who succeeded in suppressing an ancient privilege of wealthy families marked a historic turning point for the town, favored by the accession of a wide range of families of the "*borgesato.*"

And if I consider the results of the administrative elections of 1956 an emblematic fact of the process of evolution of the times and of the changed mentality of the people, I do not believe it is an error of interpretation; but the evolution of the times proceeded slowly and gradually, so much so that from immediately after the above date the administration of the town continued to be a privilege of the rich. In fact, the Mayors alternated: Dr. Gaspare Tamburello, called to manage the town by Scythian plebs mandate, who remained in office for a year. Then he was followed by a management commissioner until the elections of 1946, in which Mayor Don Crispino Ippolito was elected, who completed his mandate. From 1952 the administration passed to Cav. Nicolò Tamburello, with whom a centuries-old privilege ended in 1956.

The works of public utility and the work plans implemented in the decade 1946-56 gave impetus to the rebirth phenomenon of the Poggiorealese population. And among these, the one that gave people the most pressing push towards innovation and appetite for the cultural influences of advanced and civilized environments was when water entered the homes. The foundations of this important historical provision were laid with the deliberation of November 5, 1950, when the Municipality signed a contract with E.A.S., in agreement with the other consortium municipalities to use the water from Montescuro. And so on May 18, 1953, thanks to the solicitations of the incumbent administrators aimed at removing any bureaucratic blocks, usually slow especially when it comes to public utility works, also completed the water and sewerage network, with the inauguration of running water in the houses.

The entire population hailed the event as the grace of Heaven. The families were relieved of water shortages, especially during the summer, and from the torturous shifts under the scorching sun to fill a pitcher of water at the various sources that existed then.

The benefit of running water in the homes was of historical importance because it changed what had still been a primordial life system, vastly improving the hygiene of the person, guaranteeing a healthier and more civilized life. Toilets were built, which led to the abolition of the cesspools - which were even then a privilege of the rich - of the "*càntaru*," and of the stable, the toilets of the poor people. The urinals were no longer emptied in the streets that were dusty in summer and muddy in winter and the rains were not expected to clean the streets to make the air more breathable, which on the hottest days became heavy and unpleasant.

The following should also be remembered: the renovation of the Town Hall (resolution of January 15, 1950), which was enlarged and set up in 1955; the furnishing of the council hall and the mayor's office was arranged for the occasion; the sale of the theater for film projections; the establishment of a public telephone office (resolution of June 3, 1951); the establishment of a regional agricultural school, which in a town with a purely agricultural economy was considered providential and of primary importance. Unfortunately, this enthusiasm was betrayed in the coming years, because the school proved to be a measure of patronage and operational only on paper. Another initiative that confirmed the new face of Poggioreale, which was more demanding of cultural and recreational distractions, was the establishment of an equipped sports center that the administration of the time implemented, enthusiastically welcoming the initiative of a large number of young students of the time.

Its establishment allowed youth to promote recreational sports activities during festivities and on Sundays. In fact, there were soccer games, skeet shooting competitions, and many other events that involved the entire population. But above all the initiative proved fruitful, educational, and formative for the youth, in the sense that sports activities not only favor the year-long development of the body, but contribute to the processes of personality development from a human, cultural, and social point of view, enhance skills for completing and internalizing tasks until the achievement of adequate goals relating to education and aging.

And finally there was the restoration of the fair (resolutions of May 9, 1948 and March 6, 1949) with different characteristics than in the past, when the holiday fell on the days of the dead (November 1-2). The date was set at August 24-25 of each year. The livestock fair took place in the peripheral area of the town above the Poggioreale-Camporeale Road, while that of merchandise was held in Piazza Elimo and in Corso Umberto I. The

Reinstatement of the fair offered the population the opportunity to meet families and allowed the young people to enjoy the recreational events that were held for the occasion. The festive atmosphere and the participation of families from neighboring towns offered the privilege of promoting human, social, and cultural growth. Even today the celebration finds different cultural spaces under the name of Poggiorealese week. The livestock fair has not been held for many years, and that of commodities has shown signs of a gradual and slow regression since the earthquake of 1968, also due to the evolution of time and the change of lifestyle habits. It has become a faded presence and occasion to carry out cultural and recreational events more suited to the clever needs of our time.

Finally, the access roads to farms were improved in relation to an increase in mechanical equipment, which in that period began to be acquired by the families of the wealthiest farmers.

The elections began in June 1956 after the expiry of the mandate of the administration in office. In the preliminary meetings between the representatives of the parties, the socialists and the leftist independents, to compete with the list of the liberal party, they tried to reach an agreement with the Christian Democracy, but the negotiations failed and the socialists with the leftist parties drew up their own list, calling on Ins. Vincenzo Caronna to represent them, who gladly accepted, probably also due to a dispute with the outgoing mayor who was running again. He had been part of the previous administration and had resigned from the office of consultant because he dissented with the Mayor's work. Caronna resolutely accepted the challenge and managed to dispel a privilege that had lasted since the town's origins. The left won the elections and Ins. Caronna held the office of Mayor for two consecutive terms from June 1956 to December 1964, with the exception of a vote of no confidence in July 1959, when the secretary of the local section of the socialist party, Mr. Giuseppe Ippolito, took office as first citizen until the expiry of his mandate in November 1960. And in the electoral competition that followed immediately afterwards, Ins. Caronna again took up the office of Mayor, favored at that time by the Milazziano movement (u.s.c.s.) that garnered a lot of support in the Poggiorealese "*borgesato*."

The period from 1956 to 1964 characterized the town's administrative qualities with initiatives that connoted, in some respects, the ideological extraction of the administration in office: the solicitations to the government for the approval of the draft law on the pension of sharecroppers and direct farmers; the extension of unemployment benefits to those registered in special registries, equal pay between males and females for equal work; the solicitations to the government for granting a pension to elderly and needy veterans; Resolution no. 27 of August 25, 1956 for the Cautalì road; the pressures to the *Cassa del Mezzogiorno* to finance the work of completing the sewerage network; a program of initiatives aimed at raising awareness among the relevant political bodies for measures in favor of the weakest social classes.

The reflections of this epochal emancipation from ancient forms of social oppressions, supported by the peoples' more interested participation in political life, then assumed the character of antagonistic outburst and rift between families and relatives to the point that some forms of human and social aggregation were affected. These lacerations that remained at the level of party position without however deeply affecting the basic affective structure of the whole community reached more exasperated levels in the electoral competition of 1964, when another young teacher, Giovanni Maniscalco, strongly favored by many other young students and professionals, children of farmers, eager to change and give impetus to broader initiatives for the social, economic, and cultural growth of Poggioreale, as well as supported by the forecasts of a broad consensus of the families of farmers, as he himself was the son of a farmer, families who had become aware that things had changed and that it would be absurd to continue to caress old sympathies, began conflicting with Caronna as an exponent of the Christian Democracy. The competition was fought with the open participation of all the citizens of both parties. With the ballots having been cast, Christian Democracy prevailed with Maniscalco as Mayor. He became the top protagonist of the town's administrative life from December 1964 to July 1975, that is, for two consecutive terms, the duration of which crossed the decade due to the earthquake of January 14, 1968.

In this decade, with the exception of the disturbing economic, psychological, and moral upheaval that struck the population following the sudden and disastrous earthquake, space was given to cultural initiatives that favored human and social encounters and gave impetus to the processes of evolution of our people who, aware of their rights, made their presence felt in all the manifestations aimed at achieving better living conditions and respect for the dignity of the person. And in this regard, we must recall the protest aimed at sensitizing the national and regional government to the promotion of interventions for the development of more profitable and intensive agriculture. Prompted by this obvious need, the administration contacted the other 19 municipalities concerned and the remediation consortium of the upper and middle Belice in order to agree together on a plan of interventions designed to raise the agricultural context from its undeveloped condition. This led to the so-called march of hope in January 1965, which ended in a conference in Roccamena of all the municipalities of the area, in the presence of national and regional authorities. And here not only experts took the floor in the debate, but also our farmers, underlining their stagnant situation and pointing out the tools necessary for relaunching the agricultural economy. The foundations were laid that led to the construction of large, substantial structures for a real development of crop transformations, such as the construction of the Garcia Dam, the electrification of the countryside, the arrangement and intensification of roadways, the creation of cooperative wineries, reforestation, and more. The cultural and recreational initiatives were increased by the administration: the placement of the Christmas tree in the center of Piazza Elimo was a novelty that, at the moment of the distribution of panettone and toys to poor children, prompted the participation of a large segment of the population; the collaboration of the Municipality in the feast of the Patron Saint, St. Anthony of Padua which, with the assumption of some expenses worked to make the holiday more interesting with the presence of famous singers. All these occasions favored the influx of people from nearby towns, as well as the scheduling of soccer tournaments, the automotive gymkhana in the old Piazza Elimo organized by a special commission, stimulating a festive atmosphere that everyone could feel; the establishment of the national Elimo poetry prize that was created on the initiative of the "Teatro Amateur" group founded by Prof. Gigi Cangialosi, a young man in that period time of so many cultural initiatives, in concert with Mayor Maniscalco and sponsored by the Municipality. This initiative brought prestige to the small agricultural town of Poggioreale, because the award ceremony gathered people of great renown and culture at the Municipality, including Prof. Giorgio Santangelo, full professor of Italian literature at the University of Palermo, Giusto Monaco, full professor of Latin literature at the University of Palermo, Mario Martelli of the University of Florence, Nicolò Mineo of the University of Catania, and civil and military authorities.

 And for the occasion that usually fell on the days of the fair and Poggioreale week, collective painting exhibitions were organized which featured the presence of famous artists such as Fertitta, Gianbecchina, with the cycle of bread, Madè with that of art and crafts and others including Rosa Balestrieri with her magnificent folk singing, the Massimo choir, the band of the Carabinieri, in short a rich program of recreation and culture which, in addition to the Mayor having expressed a particular versatility for these initiatives as the helm of the administration of the time, interpreted the matured needs of a population that had come a long way in the long passage between one civilization and another; but which also felt the need to communicate, at an unconscious level, with others in order to maintain the human and social relationship that began to give imperceptible signs of thinning, especially in the transfer from the slums to the new center.

From July 3, 1975 to June 1, 1985, the mayors of the town alternated between Ins. Vincenzo Caronna and Ins. Giovanni Maniscalso. The former ended his third term on June 24, 1980; the latter ended his third electoral term in June 1985. These two were the protagonists of the administrative history of Poggioreale for just under a third of a century. Together with their councils of the respective administrations, they had to face the problems of the complex and intrigued machine of reconstruction, which has lasted over time and up to the present day with phases of stopping and slow recovery, especially in the first years due to the overlapping and stradlling of regulations that had an impact and created confusion in the bureaucratic applicative process.

From June 1, 1985 to May 20, 1990 and from May 21, 1990 to February 22, 1994, Poggioreale saw Mr. Gaetano Salvaggio serve two consecutive electoral terms as Mayor. His administration was dissolved early in the last term due to some incoherencies in the adoption of the general regulatory plan.

Gaetano Salvaggio was the first elected Mayor in the new Poggioreale.

This is also a historic date that deserves to be remembered.

With Mayor Salvaggio, the monopoly of administrative management of the two exponents was interrupted: that, stated with great approximation, of the center-left and the other of the center or center-right, with the support of fringes of the population which were not particularly politically engaged.

The term monopoly expresses only temporality and is not an expression of dissent from the long administrative alternation of the two mayors mentioned above; on the contrary, the alternation of opposite poles in politics is a positive fact and the reconfirmation of a candidate in multiple mandates is a sign and proof of work worthy of trust.

In the nine years or so of the administration represented by Mayor Salvaggio, work on the reconstruction of the town continued and public works of great artistic and monumental interest were started and for the most part completed. The following are noteworthy: Piazza Elimo by the architect Prof. Paolo Portoghesi in neoclassical style, a real architectural jewel intended to be a meeting place of all the inhabitants, a failed aim considering it is always deserted except when shows are organized; the frescoes of the council hall by the Florentine architect Paolo Malfanti; the section of road connecting the town with the Palermo-Sciacca expressway; the consolidation work of the

Agosta house of the earthquake-stricken village turned into a museum of the finds of the archaeological zone of Mount Castellaccio, already expropriated by the Municipality, and of the ethnoanthropological museum.

Although at that time there was no project for the recovery and consolidation of some sites of the ancient town, the responsible administration in those years anticipated a program that began to take shape, always at the level of initiatives to carry forward by successive administrations. Finally, the gift that this administration made to its fellow citizens should not be ignored: a nativity scene of great artistic value, in Murano glass designed by the famous painter and sculptor Pippo Madè from Palermo, whose works exhibited in all the galleries of the world convey his religiosity and bond with his roots.

The nativity scene consists of 17 large characters, with proportions varying from 30 to 90 centimeters. The characters were made in the glassworks of Murano with the "*mano volante*" (freehand) technique. Every year during Holy Christmas, a beautiful nativity scene is arranged in the Mother Church that inspires awe and wonder in the visitors who pause to admire it.

After a commissioner's administration from March 17 to May 26, 1994, following the administrative elections of the same date, Mrs. Caterina Tusa was elected Mayor and served until the end of her term of office on May 26, 1998.

Caterina Tusa was the first female Mayor of the town, called to manage, together with the members of the Council and the Board, the administration of the Municipality.

The Municipality's acts show that even in the context of routine activities, the administration showed particular attention to the problems of solidarity and public social utility, including home care for the elderly activated in 1995, monthly financial assistance to certain families of particular need, the provision of contributions to associations carrying out social, cultural, and religious activities. Among the cultural activities already implemented by the previous administrations, for example films chosen within the Cinematographic Review *Contro-Visione-Il cinema della memoria* (films of memory); another manifestation of this sensitivity was the celebration of the 30th anniversary of the earthquake of the Belice Valley, with mass held in the square of the old Poggioreale, officiated by the Archbishop of Palermo and the Bishop of Mazara. A predilection that is essentially an aspiration to save some of the sites and places of the historic city for the citizens, so that they can reuse them for various events and activities and at the same time preserve their memory. In fact, in the three-year plan of Public Works 1998-2000, a project was included, approved with a specific resolution of March 27, 1998 concerning the consolidation and functional recovery of the old Church of St. Anthony, the Morso-Naselli palace, the trough, and some sites of the old town.

Other initiatives of the administration related to the maintenance of internal and external municipal roads, the completion of the cultural center, hydrogeological work to protect the town, the completion of the lifting-water systems from the wells in the "Pili" district.

After the expiry of Mayor Tusa's term, in May 1998 the engineer Pietro Vella was elected Mayor.

Currently a few months before the reappointment, within the framework of the work program for the population, the current administration seems to have become sensitive to policy aimed at laying the foundations for a future strengthening of resources in the wine sector, which has a priority role within the economy of the local population today.

One such example is Resolution no. 131, with which the General Council entrusted an external professional with the feasibility study and technical advice for the establishment of the DOC label (Controlled Denomination of Origin) in favor of the wine products of our land. Other actions include the Municipality's membership in the *National Wine City Association* that promotes initiatives aimed to enhance wines at national and international level; the projects that are part of the financing of the *Pact of the Belice Valley agriculture* for an investment of 5,037 million in favor of the wine sector of our territory; the determined, but failed action, carried out in concert with the other Municipalities of Belice so that the irrigation works of the right and left Belice basin were included in the financing; the annual interventions against the Remediation Consortium 2 and the prefecture of Palermo to ensure the supply of water from the Garcia Dam for irrigation use in the summer period. All these efforts are the expression of a great plan to be valued in the context of a town with a purely agricultural economy.

Other interventions in the area include: the paving of the Mother Church, the water purification system of the wells ("Pili" district), the consolidation of the southwest side, sections E1 and F1 based on a loan granted by the Regional Council of the Territory and Environment according to the Italian Decree Law of June 11, 1998 (urgent interventions program); the assignment to architect Portoghesi to draw up the design for the construction of a fountain in the square in front of the Church of St. Anthony; the extraordinary maintenance of the elementary and middle schools, the extraordinary maintenance of the municipal building, the maintenance of widespread public green areas entrusted to 20 hired workers, subject to financing for socially useful works; other socially useful services beyond the routine ones include that of remote support and assistance for people who live alone and lack self-sufficiency, and finally the maintenance works of internal and external roads, the latter including both Cautalì piccolo and Cautalì grande.

And in ending the list of Mayors who have followed one another from the fall of fascism to the present day, it should be specified that, since this is recent history whose facts have been and are experienced by protagonists who are still alive, those who have assumed the burden of tracing the historical profile of their own town must use great caution and adhere to the reporting of the facts as shown by the documented data, especially in the case of the operation of municipal administrations, whose elections in a small town are always the result of conflicts of interest, ideology, trust or mistrust, sympathy and antipathy, friendship or enmity and so on. In this case, the work of the historian, which is not only to record the facts or the work of an administration as it appears in the documents, but also to give the reasons for the facts themselves and to evaluate their positivity or negativity from a human, social, cultural, political, and economic profile, could seem unfaithful to the commitment undertaken. Then the quotation of a passage from The Napoleonic Ode (*Il Cinque Maggio*) by Manzoni seems most appropriate, which in retracing the undertakings of Napoleon Buonaparte, at a certain point asks:" ... was it true glory? The future generations will deem the difficult judgement!".

Hence, my future readers will be the ones to reimagine the recent history of Poggioreale in all its positive and negative aspects while respecting reality, fully detached from their emotions and in full respect of all the historian's skills.

XXV - FROM THE EARTHQUAKE OF JANUARY 14, 1968 TO THE RECONSTRUCTION OF THE NEW TOWN

January 14, 1968 was a Sunday, a freezing-cold Sunday. Poggioreale woke up covered in snow, surprised by the unusual landscape in the morning: the roofs of the houses, the streets, the countryside, the trees were covered in a white cloak. A deep silence prevailed, not even interrupted by the bells announcing the hour of the "*Padre Nostro*" (Our Father). From time to time we could hear the twittering of the sparrows who, numbed by the cold, were perched by the gratings of the balconies and terraces in search of food, prompting the sensitivities of generous children who, upset by their strangled peeps and cheeps of suffering, threw breadcrumbs and various grains. Unfortunately, in addition to the generous children there were also some cynical and wicked adults who were pleased to take advantage of the birds' misfortune to set traps and capture them.

A Sunday different from the others was expected, perhaps more cheerful, more intimate, with more gatherings: the novelty of snow - which is very rarely seen here - was welcomed by the people with particular joy. The delighted children pressed their noses on the windows, emanating the happiness that the sight of the snow gave their small hearts exulting with joy. Others worked to collect the snow in dishes to make a granita or eat it with the cooked wine that the housewives had preserved from the previous harvest for occasional uses. Later in the morning the children came out into the streets and had fun throwing snowballs or building snowmen. A great deal of wood was burned to conquer the cold and the family gathered around the burning embers in an atmosphere of intimacy and affectionate warmth, while the woman of the house was busy preparing a piping hot soup, meat stew, or a tasty frittata of eggs and potatoes, and everything at lunch would be accompanied by a nice glass of restorative wine. The chimneys of the houses filled the air with smoke, the dark and shady sky was occasionally torn by the sun's rays which, penetrating among the clouds, brought momentary relief to the birds and all the creatures of the countryside; the peasants looked out and with satisfaction pronounced that ancient proverb that says: "*Sotto la neve pane, sotto l'acqua fame*", meaning that it was better to have snow that slowly supplied the plants with water, than a deluge of rain that caused them to suffer.

The intense cold with rain and sleet had lasted a few days, but no one could have foreseen that at lunchtime on that quiet Sunday, the tragedy of the Poggiorealese population and the other towns destroyed by the earthquake would have been unleashed.

Many families were eating their Sunday lunch, others had finished and were still around the table between one conversation and another, enjoying their time together, when suddenly the earth was struck with an 8.0 magnitude earthquake, violently shaking the houses: the plates jumped up from the tables, the doors vibrated, the chests of drawers and chairs oscillated, crevices opened in the walls, mules and horses screamed and wailed, chickens escaped, squawking with open wings, dogs were barking and you could hear the desperate cries of the terrified people pouring into the streets, the clearings, and the nearby countryside. After these sudden scenes of panic, between sobs and words of encouragement, especially from the groups of men showing courage, to the turmoil and crying, silence suddenly reigned, as if everyone wanted to listen and anticipate what would happen next. Taking advantage of the momentary calm, many people went back inside their homes to grab their valuables, some clothing and shawls to shelter from the cold; but after about an hour another 7.0-degree shock on the Mercalli scale struck, driving all those into the street who had unknowingly challenged the danger. Meanwhile, the commander of the Carabinieri station arranged rescue services and he himself, accompanied by Mayor Maniscalco, walked the streets of the town inviting people to leave their houses and meet up with the other groups of people who had been invited to stay just outside the town in the "porta" area. At about 5:00 p.m. another seven-degree shock came followed by smaller aftershocks that made the population worry, entering a state of anguish; they believed that everything was over forever. It grew dark, the cold became more penetrating, help was delayed, even if the police forces, firefighters, and the prefecture had been alerted in good time.

The repetition of the aftershocks in short intervals increased the state of confusion of the people who, overcome by panic and discouragement, were overwhelmed by uncontrolled outbursts of tears, repeating prayers to God and the Saints or expressing insolent manifestations of outrage to nature and the evil forces which had fiercely struck down a population destined to live a life of suffering for centuries, struggling to survive; a population for which time had stopped and over time all the processes of social, civil, and economic evolution had been tested; a population forgotten by God, by the heads of government, by history. In fact, the poor agricultural economies of the Belice Valley, which were finally beginning to wake up from their long torpor characterized by barriers to cultural and economic underdevelopment, the feudal-type housing structures that did not conform to the more sophisticated hygienic standards of a civil dwelling, were erased and reduced to ruins.

The first fires were lit on the outskirts of the town, around which the distorted faces crowded of women, of children trembling from the cold under a flap of a coat or shawl hanging from their mother's shoulders, faces of men with an absent stare, precisely from those who, dumbfounded and morally destroyed, emit deep sighs of anger and consternation together.

Faced with the unleashing of the forces of nature, man becomes aware of his fragility, the limits of his ability to dominate, and the precarious existence of all beings on the planet. In similar circumstances he remains silent, does not comment, but suffers in silence, hoping in divine Providence and lamenting the loss of those miserable resources that he had managed to build between hardships and slow, tiring efforts. Strange omens stirred in his mind: the worse is feared in these moments of despair and uncertainty.

The cold became more and more biting, other bonfires were lit, the old women with their backs bent struggled to stand and were waiting for the buses that the prefecture had sent to Poggioreale and where children, the elderly, women, and the poor would take their places first. It was 10:30 p.m. when the buses arrived in the area of the campfires, where most of the families had gathered; others had left by car to many areas of the nearby countryside, while a small part had travelled to their children or relatives who for work reasons had moved to other cities.

The silence of the night was occasionally interrupted by the murmur of people praying, by the cries of nursing children, cradled by the tired arms of their mother, by the chatter of some isolated group of men exchanging words of hope that everything was already over.

What futile hope! At 12:30 a.m. on January 15, a 5.0 magnitude shock stirred from the bowels of the earth to disturb those few moments of pause, erasing from everyone's mind any vague intentions of returning home, followed by silent longings for the restoration of everyday life. Ideas and suggestions were devoured by fear and the shock was considered a premonition for those who wanted to punish the discomforts of the cold and the night with insane resolutions and defy the danger of death; and it would have been certain death if many had not been firmly dissuaded by the forces of order, and the wisdom of people accustomed to pondering every decision even and above all in circumstances of turmoil and mental and organizational confusion.

In fact, only about two hours later (2:30 a.m.), a powerful 8.0 magnitude quake on the Mercalli scale shook the earth again: chills of fear mixed with those of the cold; the obsessive fear of earthquakes violently penetrates the body and spirit with more or less destabilizing repercussions depending on the responses given by the sensitivities of each person. And half an hour later, the fatal 9.0-degree shock. The screams of the women, the anguished cries of the children rose so high they feared being swallowed up by the earth, which dancing under their feet, caused unbelievable psychological lacerations.

The images of these terrifying scenes cannot be described in words, and only those who have lived through such dramatic moments are able to understand what it feels like: the fellow townspeople were looking for each other, they embraced family, relatives, friends, and enemies with a spirit of love and solidarity, it seemed like an embrace of farewell or one of joy at finding each other still alive after the immense danger they had witnessed with their eyes wide open during the very long seconds of the earth's overwhelming shaking.

The roar booming the air in the middle of the night, like the deafening and cavernous voice of a gigantic monster that wakes after a long slumber to tear the earth's crust from its bowels, the oscillation of the trees and prickly pear plants until they touch you, the great dust rising in the middle of the night from the collapsing roofs and so many perimeter walls of houses and churches, the darkness competing to destroy the psychological balance of every inhabitant up to the torment of their soul and body for several hours.

Between scenes of fear and heartbreaking screams alternating with deep silences, we reached the dawn of January 15th. The eyes of our fellow citizens were turned to the town, and seen from afar it appeared intact; after all, even today after 30 years, those who observe it from afar have the impression that the old town is still there, sad and disconsolate waiting for its inhabitants who fled to other shores, those hoping to seize the opportunity to separate from a past full of hardships and misery.

Many people, encouraged by the impression they had, wanted to return to their homes to recover clothes, precious items they had forgotten, important documents such as property titles, as well as to recover mules and beasts and work tools, but everyone was forbidden to go: it was dangerous to move among those seriously affected houses with collapsed roofs.

Meanwhile, portable radios gave news of the other completely destroyed towns: Gibellina, Montevago, Santa Margherita Belice, Salaparuta had been razed to the ground, hundreds of dead, many wounded, many towns partially destroyed and all converging in the Belice Valley, the epicenter of the earthquake. The true ordeal of the Poggiorealese and all the citizens of the affected towns began from that precise moment. During the day, between the

Photo 34 - Earthquake-stricken people around a supply truck

repetition of continuous aftershocks, the military placed a tent city on the "floor of stone" where some groups of Salaparuta had been hosted together with our villagers. This location turned out to be unsuitable and very unhealthy, because with the rain the ground became sludge and the area was exposed to the cold and humidity.

Those who owned a car preferred to use it for themselves and their family, rather than going to sleep in the tents where the people were packed together like canned sardines. Given the discomfort of those affected and at the request of the families, the authorities decided to move the tent city to the area of Sirignano. The earthquake victims who had chosen to settle in areas not far from their towns and especially those of Poggioreale, where many houses had collapsed but despite having suffered partial damage (broken roofs and perimeter walls), allowed – although not without serious risk - to recover furnishings, furniture, linen, work equipment, and many other objects. These tent cities were quite uncomfortable for the same reasons as the first tent city: isolation, cold, humidity, mud, the spread of influenzas. Before the tent city was turned into a hospital, the prefecture moved it to the sports field in the city Alcamo. Poggioreale's survivors stopped here, with the exception of many families who preferred the shelters in various other areas to the tent city.

They were days of full of disbandment, of great organizational confusion that so much disaster put thousands of families out in the streets in only a few moments: they had lost everything and suddenly found themselves beggars crowding among the trucks of food or in lines behind the field kitchens set up by the military in order to feed themselves and have a hot drink or, even more humiliating, they were forced to make their way through the crowd, pushing and shoving merely for a blanket and perhaps a coat which in the confusion were thrown to the hungry crowd, like when a shepherd throws pieces of hard bread to the dogs who, hungry, contend with growling for the food and desperately jumping into the air to catch something.

Roberto Ciuni of *Giornale di Sicilia* first reached the areas affected by the earthquake, writing: "The scale of the tragedy is much larger than can be described. It is not just a question of rebuilding towns, here the human fabric that history, understood as the Sicilian peasant civilization, has generated around the three cells has been crushed: home, stable, and hoe." And Giuseppe Carlo Marino, in the introduction to the book *1968 Terremoto in Sicilia* (1968 Earthquake in Sicily), said: "The tragic contingency highlights structural evils that do not lie in the precarious bowels of the Earth, but belong to the events of the people and the secular structure of their reality of coexistence... it has been written very appropriately that what has happened... is above all a peasant tragedy... Agriculture in crisis with many stories of oppression and mafia. Now it is time to understand that the consequences of the catastrophe must be addressed, bearing their deep and ancient causes in mind... The shame of their permanence touches at least Italy and Europe."

And speaking of the consideration that many families have lost everything and nothing with the earthquake, the journalist Giorgio Frasca Polara used the expression: "'They have murdered misery.' If there had been different socio-economic factors, the earthquake would have caused less damage; the houses collapsed as if they had been made of papier-mâché... the lack of maintained roads forced the use of helicopters to take the wounded to the equipped hospitals... that is why the earthquake was a disgrace that was merely added to the other one that had lasted centuries."

The people of the Belice Valley were aware of their living conditions and began to make their voices heard; they had already protested, pointing to interventions to defeat poverty, proof of which was the march of hope organized by many municipalities of the valley to protest against the absenteeism of the national and regional government. The Poggiorealese farmers, at the urging of the Mayor then in office and tired of suffering the bitterness of seeing their children set off in search of work, made their presence felt in that protest with targeted interventions and supported by lively, hot determination.

The aspiration to relaunch the economy and the rejection of inhibitory and tacitly suppressed constraints had matured in the consciousness of the people and took the form of life goals for which they had to fight. Some transformations had already been initiated in dedicating land to intensive crops by planting vineyards, the need for cultivating vegetables was evident, but there was a lack of infrastructure and water for these transformations to take place. So the conditions already existed to sensitize the governing bodies to create the infrastructure and encourage the population to emerge from the tunnel of underdevelopment, to promote forms of cooperation and work opportunities, as well as better living conditions. "Along with ancient monuments, the earthquake destroyed a fragile world of early achievements and hopes, the forms and structures imposed by a struggle of the people of Western Sicily against the ancient profiles of disorder and abandonment, the new profiles of dams and schools and houses and industries, just designed on the horizon of the future.

The Italian Republic must pay its centuries-old debt to Sicily immediately and without delay," Felice Chilanti wrote in an article of the newspaper.

In truth, these expressions arose from a state of affairs and suggested the emotional state of the moment, almost as if from the disgrace there was a desire not only to see the failure of the first development achievements, but also the prodromes of social, human, and economic redemption.

The government of Rome, on the other hand, suggested the disintegration of families with an immediate measure that encouraged emigration: it offered a free one-way ticket to all families and young people who wanted to leave their land for any destination, as long as it was beyond the Strait of Messina. Some social workers even wandered among the earthquake victims to urge them to leave, given that the prospects for recovery and reconstruction were projected into the distant and not immediate future. The loudspeakers insisted: "You have to leave, passports and travel for free; what are you doing staying in the tents in the mud and the cold? What will happen tomorrow? You can't stay here like this with your arms outstretched."

Thile finding consensus in some Poggiorealese families, these suggestions had no place in the majority of the population that had interpreted the suggestion to emigrate as a pretext by government officials to get rid of the refugees.

The families said no to emigration and considered the decision to leave unjust, because leaving would have meant abandoning everything; their life had been lived in Poggioreale and they had clung to that rudimentary home that had been destroyed, to that piece of land that was the result of years of hard work, to that part of the sky that opens between Monte Castellaccio, Felice, and the front coast of S. Margherita Belice, to that usual landscape that opens from the town to the south with hills and places rustic houses, olive groves, and landmarks and connotations of a landscape so familiar to us. The Poggiorealese replied, "This is where our fathers, peasants, craftsmen, daily workers, merchants have lived, we were born here and we will rebuild our lives here."

Some families departed out of despair and urged by the free offer of the journey. The exodus had Australia as its destination, where a community of Poggiorealese lived and still lives which is even more numerous than their town of origin. Some fled to Germany and Switzerland, which had been the European regions most affected by the migratory flows of young people from Poggioreale after the war, and Northern Italy. Only 173 inhabitants left the town after the earthquake, a limited number compared to the exodus that occurred in other earthquake-stricken towns and compared to the exodus of our fellow citizens in 1971, consisting of 333 people, which considerably reduced the demographic consistency of our town.

Giuseppe Avvenevole, an illiterate peasant from Poggioreale, but a vernacular poet and author of various compositions on events and manifestations of peasant life, captured the drama of the earthquake in terms of its psychological effects, emotional states, underlining the scenes of panic and terror in the light of a sensitivity that penetrates the evolutionary spirit of the tragedy:

Onnipotente dio dunami aiuto	Almighty God help me,
Sugnu poeta e mi sentu dispotu	I am a poet and I feel the need,
Di quantu cosi mali aiu vidutu	How many things I have seen
Fazzu sti parti di lu tirremotu.	I write these verses on the earthquake.
Lu tirrimotu lu sintia diri	I had heard about the earthquake
Picchì a me patri lu sintia cantari	because my father had told me about it
Allurtimata comu iù a finiri	But I also experienced
Chi puru eu ci ivi a 'ngaghiari.	how it ended.
E cu 'n ci 'ngaghia nessunu ci criri	And whoever hasn't felt it, can't believe
Lu tirrimotu chi dannu po fari	The damage the earthquake can cause
Cu 'n avia sordi a lu putiri	Those lacking money
Ristai mezzu li strati addumannari.	Were left on the streets as beggars.
Ora vi dicu quannu fu lu 'nfernu	Now I'll tell you of the hell
A li 14 jnnarua mezziornu	On January 14th at noon
Penzu chi n'aiutà lu Patri Eternu,	I believe the Eternal Father helped us,
la prima scossa la desi di jornu.	As the first shock came during the day.
Niscemu fora cu lu suli 'mpernu	We all came out with the sun high
Pi talari cu c'era dda attornu	To see who was around
'n c'era nuddu chi si stava fermo	no one was standing still
pariamu tutti cu lu capu stornu	we all seemed totally bewildered
e mentri sona allarmi la sirena	and while the sirens of Salaparuta
di Salaparuta e Gibellina	and Gibellina were sounding
fu 'mmiraculu di Santa Maddalena	it was a miracle of Saint Magdalene
'n fari tutti 'na morti mischina	that we didn't die a horrible death
lu popolu sfollava a forti lena	the people crowded praying
priannu sempre a Santa Catarina	always to Saint Catherine
ogni pirsuna pi lu scantu trema	every person trembling for the fear
vidennu chi s'arresta a la ruvina	seeing those stopped at the ruins
'n c'era né gniuranti e mancu spertu	there were neither the ignorant nor experts,
tutti morti di scantu e di paura	all dead for fear and dread

cu 'n fici prestu a nesciri all' apertu	those who did not make it out quickly remained
ristai 'nsirragghiatu 'nta li mura.	trapped within the walls.
Si sdirruparu la stessa jurnata	Montevago and Santa Margherita
Muntivau e Santa Margherita	Fell on the same day
Lu tirrimoto vinni all 'impinzata	The earthquake came out of nowhere
Cu persi robba e cu persi munita	Some lost goods and some coins.
La populazioni spaventata	The frightened population
Ia gridannu con vuci smarrita	went shouting with harsh voices
Cu curia a pinninu e cu a muntata	Those who ran downhill and those uphill
Ognunu pi sarvarisi la vita.	Each to save his life.
E di Puggiuriali chi v'è diri	And of Poggioreale what to say
Ancora nuddu vulia scappari	Still no one wanted to leave
A la scurata comu iu a finiri	Towards the evening, it then wound up
Ch 'ognunu 'n sappi chiù dunni pigghiari.	That no one knew where to go any more.
Comu si vittiru li mura trimari	As the walls were seen trembling
Prestu curreru li carabineri	Soon the police intervened
Tutti li genti ficiru sfullari	And all the people were ordered
A ordini spressu di lu briateri	To move by the brigadier
'n si cerca né roba né denari	none were allowed to look for things or money
cu abbrazza figghi e cu abbrazza mughieri	some embraced children and some their wives
prestu ni 'ncumingiamu alluntanari	soon we began to move away
cunsidirati cu quali pinseri.	considering with what thoughts.
Subitu cominciaru a telifunari	They he began to call
A la pulizia e a li pumperi:	the police and firefighters:
"Viniti prestusenza ritardari	"Come quick without delay
lu populu sfullà d'ogni quartieri	the people are displaced from every neighborhood
in ogni famigghia c'è lagrimi amari	in every family there are bitter tears
cu fannu chiantu e cu fannu prieri	those who weep and those who pray
a lu paisi 'n ponnu riturnari	they cannot return to the town
si sdirruparu tetti e cantuneri."	there are collapsed roofs and homes."
Di notti e notti si vittiru arrivari	In the middle of the night
Na massa di camii e curreri	Many trucks and buses arrived
Cussì n'annu vinutu a rintracciari	So they came to find us
Mezzu li stratuna e li trazzeri.	In the middle of the streets and tracks.

-159-

Lu jornu di lu 15 matina	On the morning of the 15th
Ni puttarn a la Petra 'nti l'accampamentu	They took us to the "Pietra" in camp
Truvamu li capanni e la cucina	We found the tents and the kitchen
Cuss'arnu avutu 'n pocu d'abbentu.	So we had a bit of a break.
Appena chi scurà dda siritina	As soon as it grew dark, in the evening
La terra fici un forti scutimentu	The ground shook strongly,
Dda latu sdirrupa n'a casina	Nearby a small house collapsed,
Cunsidirati chi forti spaventu.	Imagine what a strong fright.
Lu populu facia n'a ruvina	The people feared ruin
Cu facia vuci e cu lamentu	Those who shouted and those who cried,
Lu cumannanti di la disciplina	The people responsible for order
Subitu fici fari spustamentu.	Immediately arranged for their transfer.
Ni traspurtaru n'atru pocu arrassu	They moved us a little further away
Spirannu di truvari megghiu versu	Hoping to find a better place,
Lu tirrimotu chi facia fracassu	The earthquake that ruined everything
Unn'era era ci vinia appressu.	Followed us everywhere we went.
Vidennu tuttu stu populu ammassu	Seeing all the people piled up
A tutti smossi un pocu di rimorsu	Everyone had a bit of remorse
Cunsideratu lu poveru scarsu	Considering the poor without anything,
Prestuarrivau lu prontu soccorsu.	Soon emergency aid arrived.
Lu primu c'arrivau fu un parrinu	The first to arrive was a priest
Cu lu sacramentu 'nta li manu	With the monstrance in his hands,
Priamu tutti a Cristu divinu	We all pray to Divine Christ
Quantu sarvassi lu generu umanu.	To save the human race.
Lu tirrimotu batti di cuntinuu	The earthquake was constantly shaking
E dunni passa nenti resta sanu	And where it passes, nothing remains healthy,
'n sta lassannu mancu un casalino	It's not even leaving the small hamlets
macari li muntagni mette 'ngnanu.	Even the mountains are becoming flat.
Vidennu lu periculu vicinu	Seeing the danger nearby
Omini e fimmini cu la cruna 'manu	Men and women with the crown in their hands,
Priamu la Madonna e lu Bamminu	Let us pray to Our Lady and the Child
Chi duna aiutia ogni cristianu.	To help every Christian.
Avogghia di priari fortementi	I want to pray intensely
Ma 'n ci potti né Dio né Santi	But God and the Saints

Semu rimasti poveri scuntenti	Were powerless and we remained poor and sad
Cul'occhi chini e li manu vacanti.	With eyes full of tears and empty hands.
Ora vi parlu di li patimenti	Now I'll tell you about the sufferings
Chi pottimu aviri sull' istanti	That we suffered instantly:
ci sunnu 124 tenni	there are 124 tents
e ci alluggiamu 3000 abitanti.	and there are 3,000 inhabitants.
Passau lu capitanu e lu tenenti	The captain and the lieutenant passed,
n'atra cosa fu la chiù putenti	but it was even worse
chi nu truvamu né riti né branti	because there were no beds nor cots
lu ponnu dire cu era presenti	those who were there can confirm
di quantu foru li lacrimi e chianti	how many tears and weeping
Pi tutti li famigghi cuntrullari	From all the families
E vidennu lu chianti di li genti	And seeing the weeping of the people
Puru annu cominciatu a lacrimari.	They too began to cry.
E n'annu dittu: "Stativi contenti	And they told us, "Be happy.
E stu bruttu martiriu suppurtari	And this ugly martyrdom we have endured
Ora pigghiamu li pruvvidimenti	Now we take measures
Quantu chiù megghiu putiti alluggiari";	So that you can be better";
n'atra cosa megghiu ni cunsigghia	another thing they advised is
senza pinsari si 'n si travagghia lu	don't worry if you're not working
tirrimotu fa lu lenta e pigghia e tutti	the earthquakes ceased
cosi pi ariu spagghia.	with everything up in the air.
Ogni pirsuna prestu si risbigghia	Every person wakes up as soon
Appena senti scrusciu di tirragghia	As he hears the clinking of cooking wares
Curri pi fora e nun vidi dunni pigghia	And does not know what road to take
Fazza chi 'nta li mura lu 'nzinzgghia;	To avoid being blocked by walls of people;
arristau dintra tutta la mustrigghia	everything remained at home
senza pigghiari mancu n'a tuvagghia	without taking even a tablecloth,
n'alluntanamu chiù di 20 migghia	we distanced ourselves more than 20 miles
a dormiri 'nterra comu na canagghia.	to sleep on the ground like beggars.
Lu patri pi l'amuri di la figghia	The father for the love of his daughter
Ch'era 'mparata cu riti a magghia	Those who were used to sleeping in beds
Senza superba e mancu maravigghia	Without pride would not marvel
Ia addumannannu fenu e pagghia.	In asking for hay and straw.

Semu tutti scarsi di rubigghia	We have nothing
Lu friddu ancora megghiu 'napprisagghia	The cold attacks us even more
Pi risturari un pocu la famigghia	To warm the family however we can
Cu carria zucca e cu ramagghia;	There are those who grab trunks and those branches;
tutta la notti si facia vigghia a	All night long, they keep a watchful eye
terra netta e macari vagnata	sitting on the lone and maybe even wet earth,
tutti ammunzeddu comu li cunigghia	all bunched together like rabbits
priamu la Madonna Addulurata.	and we pray to Our Lady of Sorrows.
Unn 'abbastava chidda malavita	And as if it that horrible situation were not enough
A chioviri si misi dda nuttata	The rain began that night
N'acqua forti di chidda salita	A stormy rain, the type
Pi cunsari bonu 'nzalata.	That makes lettuce grow well.
Vidennu chi fu mala la partita	Seeing that the situation was worsening
Sdesimu prestu cu la matinata	We woke early in the morning,
la terra era un occhiu di crita	the ground had become sludge
e l'acqua curia a lavinata;	and the rain came down hard;
'nta lu me cori c'era na ferita	in my heart there was a wound
vidennu la famigghia 'nfruinzata	seeing my family come down with the flu,
niscivi fora cu furia ardita	I left the tent with a daring fury
e prestu addumavi 'na vampata,	which soon ignited,
lu ventu chi paria 'na calamita	the wind was biting, it was that
era prudenza di chidda agghiacciata	icy cold north wind
e agghiacciannu li manu e li ita	that froze my hands and fingers
ogni persona si sintia malata.	and every person felt sick.
Appena hann 'arriavatu li dottura	As soon as the doctors arrived,
Tutti l'hannu chiamatu a vuci lesta	Everyone called out to them with sick voices,
Senza né stufa né cummigghiatura	Without a stove for warmth or a blanket
Cu avi tussi e cu avi dulura 'ntesta;	There are those who cough and those with headaches;
lu tempu pari chi lu fici apposta	it seems like the weather did it on purpose
a fari friddu e chioveri atimpesta	to make it cold and rain like a storm,
e e si nuddu ni duna 'na risposta	and if no one gives us an answer
dumani megghiu s'incarna la festa.	tomorrow it will get even worse.
Li dottura sintennu sta priposta	Hearing this proposal, the doctors
si taliaru e scuteru la testa	look at each other and shake their heads

pinzannu la saluti quantu costa	thinking about health and how much we're paying:
"dumani assira nuddu ca ci arresta".	"tomorrow night no one shall sleep here."
Vidennu chi la cosa è di primura	Seeing that it was urgent
Si misiru a rapportu cu lu cumannu:	They communicated with the commander:
"La genti hannu a spustari cu primura:	"People must move quickly because this
picchì la frigilità fà troppu dannu.	*frailness* causes too much damage.
Veru chi s'accaddi 'nta la svintura	It is true that this misfortune happened
E ama suppurtari stu malannu	And we must endure this disease,
Cu avi tussi e cu rifriddatura	Those who cough those with a cold
E comu hannu a fari unni lu sannu".	And they do not know what to do".
Vidennu chi la cosa è d'impurtanza	Considering the immediate importance,
Subitu fu accittata la partenza	Our departure was arranged saying:
Dicennu: "unnè di nui la curanza	"It is not our fault
E bisugnamu aviri gran pacenza	And we must have much patience;
ad Arcamu c'avemu la speranza	in Alcamo we hope
di fari 'na bona permanenza	to make a better tent city,
roba 'n'arrivau n'abbunnanza	aid will come in abundance
e la spartemu senza differenza".	and we will divide it indifferently".
Lunn'umani si vitti migghiuranza	The next day there was an improvement
Chi cuminciaru a dari l'assistenza	Because they began to provide assistance,
primu hannu pinzatu pi la panza	first they filled our bellies
e doppu pi curari la 'nfruenza;	and then treated the flu;
lu nostru Presidente in circostanza	our President believed he was doing
pinzau a fari beneficenza:	charity for the occasion:
"Cu sinni voli iri alluntananza	"Whoever wants to emigrate
dunni fari megghiu residenza..."	where their residence can improve... "
Vidennu chi n'annu datu larga manu	Since they gave us a big hand,
'na pocu s'hannu fattu lu scuntrinu	some of them booked their tickets,
cu sinn'iu a Roma e cu a Milanu	those who went to Rome, those to Milan,
cu sinn'iu a Firenze, cu a Torino	to Florence, to Turin;
ma eu c'avia du muli pi li manu	but I, who had two mules for my hands,
mi tratt'inni unn'era chiù vicinu	stayed where they were closest
dicennu: "comu abbatti lu vurcanu	saying, "when this volcano stops,
minni vaiu a zappari lu jardinu".	I'm going to hoe the garden."

Lu cuntu di lu poviru viddanu	The plans of the poor peasant
Unn'arrinesci mai giustu a puntinu.	Can never quite do it,
lu tirrimotu a statu veru stranu	the earthquake was really strange
durau quasi un misi di cuntinuu	it lasted almost a month continuously.
La mala sorti di lu sicilianu	The bad luck of the Sicilian
Chi capitau stu malu distinu	Struck by this poor fate!
Semu alloggiati nt'a 'n pezzu du chianu	We are housed in a flat area
Nt'a li capanni cu lu briccialinu.	In tents placed on gravel.
Cunsidiramu n'a povera donna	Let us consider a poor woman
Stari alloggiata dintra na capanna	Who lodges inside a tent
Cu ci duna lu bustinu e cu n'a gonna	Those who give her a blouse and those a skirt,
Cu ci duna la magghia e la mutanna	Those who give her a shirt and panties
'n c'era né russuri né vriogna	there was neither redness nor shame
ogni sfollata la manu vi sparma	every person in the crowd stretches out their hand,
paremu tutti figghi di 'na mamma	like we're all children of a single mother;
e ora chi lu deboli cunfermu	and now I must confirm a confession,
vi lu ripetu tri boti lu jornu	I repeat it three times a day
chi s'unn'aiuta lu nostru cuvernu	that if our government doesn't help us,
'n c'è nessunu chi farà ritornu.	no one is coming back.
Primu priamu a chiddu di Palermu	First we turn to the one in Palermo
E a tutti l'amici c'avi attornu	And to all the friends around him,
Anzi che ura chi veni l 'ummernu	Before winter comes,
Volemu fattu lu novu riformu.	We want him to give us a roof over our heads.
Amici vi lu dicu a tutti quanti	Friends, I'll tell you all
Perdiri tutto su guai trimenti	There are terrible troubles;
avemu tutti li taschi vacanti	we all have empty pockets,
vulemu aiutu di lu Presidenti	we want the President's help.
Priamu a Cristu cu tutti li Santi	Let us pray to Christ with all the Saints
Quantu chi n'aiutassi veramenti	So that they can really help us
Fari li casi è lu chiù 'mpurtanti	Rebuild the houses it is very important,
quantu ni leva di sti patimenti.	to relieve us from these sufferings.
Lu nostru Presidenti Saragatti	Our President Saragat
E' competenti e provvidi pi tutti a	Has the competence and will take care of everyone,
tutti quanti ni rispetta a parti	everyone will respect us,

e chiddi c'avemu li casi distrutti.	we who have destroyed houses.
N'a pocu s'hanno fattu persuasi	Some persuaded themselves
Di viaggiari senza fari spisi	To emigrate for free,
E ghiri a circari terra e casi	In the search for land and houses
Ni l'Americani e ni l'ingrisi	Between the Americans and the English;
ma eu c'avia li casi chini rasi	But I, who had a full house
arristavi cu li robi misi	I stayed with the clothes I had on my back,
e si lu cuvernu fabbrica li casi	and if the government manufactures the houses
fazzu ritornu a lu me paisi	I will return to my town.
Ora chi sugnu lestu di parlari	Now that I have finished speaking
Dumannu scusa s'aiu fattu arruri	I apologize if I made mistakes
Quann'era nicu 'n potti studiari	When I was little I could not study
E sugnu rozzu puisiaturi	And I am a crude poet
E rozzamenti mi vulissi firmari	But I'd like to sign
Tantu pi sapiri l'auturi	So you will know the author:
Avvenevole Vincenzo di Puggiurriali	Avvenevole Vincenzo of Poggioreale
Aiu composto sti mali scritturi	I composed this poor poem
Scriviri 'n potti tuttu lu caminu	I could not write the entire journey
Chi sugnu vecchiu e mi trema la manu,	Because I am old and my hand trembles,
ma siddu era quarantanni primu	but it was 40 years before
facia tuttu lu romanzu sanu.	I would have told the whole story.
Benché chi di menti sugnu finu	Although my mind is refined
Ma scriviri n'unsacciu talianu	I do not know how to write in Italian
Sugnu un puvureddu cuntadinu	I am a poor farmer,
Amici vi salutu di luntanu.	Friends I salute you from afar.

The tent city of the Alcamo sports field housed about 1,000 Poggiorealese, as well as some earthquake-stricken groups from Gibellina and Salaparuta. Those staying here were distributed among the tents in families.

    The civil and military authorities carried out activities worthy of mention, for the moral and organizational support they offered with a spirit of self-denial and within the limits of the resources that day after day were made available to them to lighten the discomfort of the population and make everyday life more livable.

In fact, a better-equipped field kitchen was created; the long humiliating lines of earthquake-stricken who waited for the distribution of meals with a mess tin in hand were eliminated (see photo). Essential services were established: the postal service and the telephone service that allowed those in the tents to communicate with relatives, children, parents, distant siblings. A bus service was established that allowed the population to resume daily contacts with the evacuated town both to recover objects from partially destroyed homes and to resume field work after recovering the mules from the work animal collection centers. There were other comforts such as an electric stove, the distribution of mattresses, the availability of military showers and toilets, even if theirs were for simple accommodations until their barracks were built, the recovery of school for the children, the celebration of Holy Mass: these were all comforts and signs of a life that was beginning to recover.

In this phase of organizational discomfort, the work carried out by Mayor Maniscalco was distinguished, that of the civil and military authorities, of Dr. Francesco Mulè and Dr. Giovanni Salvaggio who made every effort to ensure assistance and relief to the injured population. In the tent city the people certainly lived a gypsy life, and above all the women felt the discomfort more than the men; indeed, various problems arose. They were continually beset by a sense of modesty, considering that daily life did not take place according to the normal limits of intimacy and personal freedom.

The aid and spirit of solidarity reached very high levels, even if a certain disorder was observed in granting offers to the recipients. In an article of the newspaper *Giornale di Sicilica*, Roberto Ciuni wrote: "International solidarity has moved; a river of trucks loaded with supplies and blankets has poured over the affected places, but it is here that the brakes of skills, of bureaucracy, of jealousy between association and association are still stuck. It is angering to see people sleeping on hay on the ground, while ten, twenty meters ahead train cars full of blankets and mattresses sit idly. And if you ask why they don't distribute them, the drivers reply that there is no order."

In other words, it was a question of coordination that had not been resolved. A central hub was required, one that everything could depend on.

Aid came from all over Italy; bodies and administrations made promises for aid, including *La Stampa* of Turin, the *Giornale di Sicilia, La Sicilia,* the Italian Red Cross, the trade union confederations, radio-TV and many other

Photo 35 - Earth-quake stricken waiting in line for a hot meal
-167-

entities. RAI-TV collected about three billion lira, the distribution of which respected the principle of privileging the towns that had been completely destroyed. Poggioreale was owed about three hundred million that the administration then in office divided among the citizens using the Rai-TV money that had instead been earmarked for social works. Help came from America with villages consisting of substantial barracks, from England, from France, from Russia, from the German and Austrian Red Cross. Many students, police, soldiers, volunteers of different nationalities mobilized to assist those affected. The State came to help with E.C.A. for all: 1,000 lire for the head of the family, 500 for his wife, 400 for the other members. The State then gave all the families a contribution of 500,000 lire and the Region gave them 200,000 for the reconstruction of farms.

And in the meantime, the basic structures for the construction of a slum began to be created: roads, a water network, electricity grid, various services. The Alcamo tent camp lasted until the summer of 1968, but the stay in the slums was very long, for some families about 15-16 years. Many children born at that time almost reached maturity without knowing a comfortable home and a civil life. Living in a shack for 16 years is a very long period in a man's life. There were all sorts of inconveniences and those who had this bitter experience remember it quite well.

The first affliction of the slums is that they were not sufficiently suitable for living decently and meeting the intimacy needs between the same members of a family and between different families, housed possibly in the same shack divided into two non-acoustically isolated accommodations. The spirit of adaptation was based on the conviction and hope that the slums had been built with a provisional character and with the prospect that the construction of the new town would soon be carried out; and instead they became stable dwellings, in which one was not free to discuss projects and initiatives among the same family members, if not without lowering their voice. In families sometimes there were conflicts between husband and wife, between parents and children; they could not vent freely, and they were forced to continuously control their reactions to avoid bringing out all the manifestations of daily life. The heat of summer that wears everyone away and generates forms of intolerance up to the limits of tolerability and the bitter cold of winter that paralyzes the body and the spirit, especially for people of a certain age, require a great willingness to adapt and not without the danger of contracting rheumatic, pulmonary, and many other diseases related to poor health in the cold seasons. And the more years passed, the more the earthquake-stricken looked to the future with attitudes of distrust and resignation together[1] due to the construction delays, the failure to determine the Municipalities that required priority interventions.

There was an urgent need for warehouses for the storage of products, in order to avoid selling the harvest to crooks who took advantage of the misfortune of others in order to increase their earnings.

It is true that mechanization had replaced animal power, but there were farmers who still used mules to travel from the town to the countryside and for some jobs. Hence the need to create stables to house the beasts. And in fact, thanks to the administration many stables and facilities were built to store the supplies of straw and hay in an area near the slums.

After the difficulties of getting settled in the early days and as people's shortcomings and needs were integrated through measures aimed at satisfying small and temporary problems of a socio-environmental nature, a rhythm of life was restored that together synthesized tradition, culture, and the mentality of the past on the one hand and radical innovations inspired by social achievements and new values on the other. After the first hard years with the new conditions of life, years of demographic decline followed (we must not forget the exodus of three hundred Poggiorealese in 1971), new demands knocked at the door of the heart which, freed from the anguish that had gripped the strongest fibers and explosively opened to seize the most radiant aspects of life, pushed our people to compare themselves with the past and stretch their arms towards the more immediate future through the aspirations of the young people to a freer life less conditioned by certain taboos that had compressed the inner and natural motions like in a tight suit. The traditions and human and social relationships were favored by the structure of the slum itself; families concentrated in wooden or iron barracks could only afford to meet with one another, chat with neighbors, exchange greetings, gossip.

The example of the parents who brought their habits of life to the barracks slowed the flight of young children towards more or less transgressive manifestations of the old values, depending on the different impact that the mass media had exerted on the developmental processes of their educational formation.

The participation in cultural and recreational events became more massive; there was a great deal of excitement for the Carnival festivities, whose party

---

[1] Father Traina Mariano, *Vale del Belice* (Belice Valley), Ed. typography "Fiamma Serafica", Palermo 1978.

was held in the gymnasium of the middle school and in the premises of the culture club which in those times was popular among professionals, students, and people of different social classes; in the late afternoon and evening they took frequent walks among friends along the new roads of the slum, where the three old bars of the evacuated town had been reconstituted. The administration of the time, as has been said, favored these new needs by promoting reconnections with organizational interventions that were more responsive to the expectations of the population.

The new face of the villagers was also favored by the resumption of agricultural work with more profitable yields and less waste of energy and time. All the farms had been mechanized by now, both small and large; the most modest of the *borgesi* could embrace the cultivation of larger areas of land with advanced and very profitable techniques thanks to the use of fertilizing products, previously unknown. In addition, the transition from an extensive crop to another intensive one reached milestones worthy of mention, also favored by the contributions that the State and Region had allocated to farmers for the recovery of their farms. The planting of vineyards intensified year by year, so much so that the most substantial revenues came precisely from the vineyards. And to conclude these reflections on life in the barracks, it must be emphasized that Poggioreale's transition from peasant civilization to the era of progress and technology was already in place as a mentality, but still ongoing in the practice of daily life.

XXVI - RECONSTRUCTION

In the immediate aftermath of the earthquake, projects were made for reconstruction that were seen dually as a rebirth of the Belice Valley from the socio-economic point of view and the reconstruction of decent and comfortable housings for all the families who had lost their homes with the earthquake. In an article published in *La Stampa* in Turin, the journalist Nicola Adelfi wrote: "Italy must not refuse its help in the most solicitous manners to a part of itself that is now under the threat of complete and definitive disintegration." In an article of *Il Giorno* of Milan, Francesco Campagna wrote: "You cannot think of reconstruction without preparing an investment plan over time that will transform the old economy of the earthquake-stricken area (grains and wine) into a new economy, integrated by verticalized agricultural products (milk, livestock products, fruit, vegetables) with manipulation and industrialization in the places." It was hoped, as the first large resource of the area, that the extraordinary interventions already planned for the irrigable areas, for the industrial development of the provinces affected by the earthquake, would be carried out and that interventions in civil works would be planned as recognition of the particularly depressed conditions of the area most affected by such a serious natural calamity.

The towns were rebuilt with all the hesitation and difficulty due to the bureaucratic processes and the slowness that characterized the development of the works, due to the presence of sometimes well-identified vices, due to the absence of pressure, and for many other reasons that it is not necessary to recall here; unfortunately, whether rebirth is still a hope or not, perhaps no longer, because these new rebuilt centers suffer a worrying demographic decline: they risk becoming small villages of the elderly.

The problem of the town's reconstruction was quite complex and so important that the population, recognizing that it did not rise to the level of advancing hypotheses or solutions on what to do, became disinterested and entrusted the work to the competent bodies. These attitudes, with the exception of some more politically engaged fringes who believed they were actively participating, made most families indifferent, resigning themselves to forcing their spirit of adaptation to the hardships of life in the barracks, perhaps confirmed by some compensatory measures, such as the free water and electricity, the exemption from municipal and state taxes, and other small awards that left them content and duped.

Several issues were discussed related to the choice of the area in which to rebuild the new towns, initially the most relevant of which was the conurbation plan of Minister Mancini of the three towns; Gibellina, Poggioreale, Salaparuta. Several meetings were held under the chairmanship of the Inspectorate-General of I.S.E.S., Engineer Luigi Corona; the meetings highlighted the advantages that the three towns would have and above all the young people because the future was of the young and not of the elderly clinging to their own rock like the Malavoglia family recalled by Verga. The elderly always showed a keen reluctance towards initiatives that would have buried habits, considered indispensable for the serene continuation of the harmonious relationship between man and the environment.

However, despite being supported by valid arguments that underlined the benefits that the inhabitants would have, such as a high school that would have prevented young people from traveling daily, the establishment of an equipped hospital, the presence of new commercial and business resources, the creation of new socio-economic structures facilitated by the impact that the larger housing center would exert on the sensitivity of political and institutional bodies with respect to villages, the initiative failed, destined to bleed out year after year. The area proposed for the conurbation was Rampinzieri, between Gallitello and S. Ninfa, but the municipalities involved did not agree for various reasons, including the distance from the land to be cultivated (for many farmers the passage from the town to the countryside was carried out on muleback); the phenomenon of attachment to the original location itself, which has been mentioned; a certain hometown pride and many other reasons that escape the writer.

According to the indications given by Father Mariano Traina in the cited work, the first Municipality that disagreed with the idea of the conurbation was Gibellina with the then-Mayor L. Corrao, who with resolutions of September 2 and 17, 1969 abandoned the I.S.E.S. project. In December of the same year, the administration ratified the decision to rebuild the town in Salinella for the facilitated connections to the Mazara-Palermo motorway and because it was more in the center of the area to which it belonged.

As for the location of Poggioreale, there is a resolution of February 1, 1968 with which the administration pronounces itself for the area of Mandria di Mezzo, a decision that anticipated the dissent of Gibellina for conurbation. This decision, which took shape with a specific deliberation, had to be supported by geological and geophysical studies that would have detected its suitability for the purposes of the reconstruction of the new town. According to the news reported in the aforementioned book by Traina, Prof. Ruggeri of the University of Palermo had undertaken to lead a team that would carry out research to ascertain which areas would be most compatible for the citizens' safety. A small amount of funding was obtained from the National Research Council, a commission was formed which included Prof. Cassinis, Prof. Jappelli, the former for geophysics and the latter for geotechnics.

But due to the student unrest of 1968, they could no longer take more time from their teaching activities, and the investigations were entrusted to two young men, Dr. Damanti and Dr. Todaro. The result of these studies highlighted a link between geological structures and seismic damage, i.e., Poggioreale had suffered less damage than Salaparuta and Gibellina and could be rebuilt in the same site instead of in Mandria di Mezzo, where due to the frequent presence of faults ascertained since 1954 by the geologists Professors De Pampilis and Marini, the choice was not advised.

The latter thesis is supported by geophysical research carried out in 1968 by Prof. Cassinis and Dr. La Torre. There were divergent opinions on the choice of the area: on the one hand, there were politically engaged people who advocated the choice of Mandria di Mezzo in the assemblies, on the other hand some representatives of wealthy families wanted the location of the new town to be in the old site, reusing the historical center of the destroyed town and the spaces that stretched from the outskirts towards the slums. The latter sent the competent authorities a report so that their proposal could be accepted on the basis of the geologists' suggestions; they even resorted to a discussion with the geologists, but every attempt was futile. The representatives of the people, out of mature ideological aversion and probably out of fear that rebuilding on the spot would maintain the privileges of the families who had their homes along Corso Umberto and in Piazza Elimo, warmly supported the transfer of the new Poggioreale. Many families, young people, and professionals were kept away from this diatribe, who could have made a thoughtful contribution for solutions which were more suited to the daily needs of an entire population.

The choice of Mandria di Mezzo was perhaps more futuristic for young people and the future developments of the town: the easy access to the Palermo-Sciacca highway and the much-vaunted Belice axis that would connect the town with the Palermo-Mazara highway, all basic prerequisites for that famous revival of the Valley which remained merely a hoped-for conquest of the earthquake-torn populations. On the other hand, the transfer would have been traumatic for all those people who had lived in the old town for a greater part of their lives: deep-rooted habits for years, affections born and fortified by time, a way of life related to the environment and based on things and people, streets, corners that hold memories and arouse nostalgia, in short, of an entire world that has supported that psychological balance which every man needs in order to live a peaceful life without worries, nor inner disturbances that stand in the way of the determination of the choices and plans of tomorrow.

The choice of Mandria di Mezzo also prevailed due to the explicit will of Engineer Corona, who on August 26, 1969 presented his plan for the approval of the Municipality. Father Traina considered that choice worse because "It swallowed with the walls alone so many billions that would have been enough to build a city." And on *Il Domani* of September 15, 1977, he wrote: "It is known that the new settlement of Poggioreale is in an inconsistent area; we know the amounts spent to first make some walls, then to make the walls of the walls, then to make the walls for the walls of the walls." He wrote about a parliamentary inquiry into the location of the new towns. Then he asked himself: "... what's the point of carrying out an investigation today?" and added: -"if Stalin had been there... if Mussolini had been there... if De Gasperi had been there, none of this would have happened."

Evidently, the controversy raised by Traina in *Il Domani* takes on the tone of the fiery protest, so much so as to recall names such as Mussolini and Stalin; in this case it is difficult to determine to what extent he presents reality with nuances of dissent, which exaggerate its aspects.

I agree that there is no doubt to the fact that the area has less fortunate characteristics than that of the old town: the air is heavier on the days with the sirocco winds and in the hot months of summer it is much more suffocating than the old town. The soil on which the land stands seems less compact in the investigations carried out by the experts who detected the presence of frequent faults; the panorama that opens up before the eyes of the population presents limited views of the landscape; the exposure of the town opens it up to the four winds that make the cold seasons harsher.

However, I think it is superfluous to continue to indicate advantages and shortcomings between the new and the old town, also because each person is a subject in and of himself and expresses favorable or negative opinions according to his own points of view. Pirandello says, "Man is one, no one, one hundred thousand," according to the different judgments that others express about him, and since these judgments are never unanimous, the well-known Sicilian writer asks himself: "What then is the true identity of each one of us?". Similarly, if we ask people about the location of the new town, the opinions differ vastly: there are those who consider it better and those worse when comparing it with the devastated town, even if the greater percentage of the population expresses its favor for the latter, perhaps for an affective fact.

Given this premise on the choice of the location of the new town, a process that gave rise to conflicting opinions and various controversies, it seems appropriate to address, summarily, the legislation that regulated the developments of the reconstruction.

The first law issued by the State to address the problems of reconstruction was Law no. 241 of March 18, 1968, converting Decree Law no. 79 of February 27, 1968. With this law, the first resources for the reconstruction of the houses were allocated after preparing the urban plans.

In the municipalities that were entirely transferred, such as Poggioreale, Salaparuta and Gibellina, since the building areas were not yet available, private individuals were not able to take advantage of the law's financing, which instead was used in the other Belice municipalities.

The law that gave rise to the actual beginning of the reconstruction was that of April 29, 1976, no. 178, obtained following the various strikes and the march on Rome of the Belice populations. Article 5 of this law called for the constitution of a commission chaired by the mayor or his delegate and composed of technicians of the Inspectorate General of the earthquake-stricken areas and four members of the Council, two of whom were elected by the minority.

The commission thus constituted envisaged the allocation of the lots, the examination of the applications and the approval of the related projects for the reconstruction of the first real estate unit, as well as the determination of the contribution. Determined based on the household and according to the costs of social housing, the contribution was issued by the head of the Inspectorate General for the areas affected by the earthquake. On March 5, 1977, the committee, formed by Ins. Vincenzo Caronna, Chairman, and the members Giuseppe Bavetta, Innocenzo Sgrò, Lorenzo Di Giovanna, Francesco Belletti, representative of the Inspectorate Giovanni Bonura, union representative, proceeded by making random drawings for the first and most substantial allocation of lots.

The first financing came in September of the same year. With Law no. 64 of August 4, 1978, the contribution was extended to other units beyond the first and for a maximum of 10 million lire. Subsequently, other laws were enacted that introduced the half-yearly indexing of the assigned contributions.

With art. 13 bis of the law of March 27, 1987, the rules that the State had issued for the reconstruction in Irpinia following the earthquake of 1980 were applied in Belice, according to which, after the dissolution of the Inspectorate, the Mayor was given the power to grant contributions.

Wanting to make some remarks about the initial blockage of the legislation which would have regulated the developments of the reconstruction, it should not be kept silent that the State was not prepared to face a natural disaster such as that of the Belice Valley: there were no adequate Civil Protection facilities; consequently, there were developments in the legislation based on the gradual experiences that the bodies responsible for the legislation were having on the shoulders of all the families, who had climbed out of their roof, had waited for 13-14 years and perhaps longer for their much-anticipated house. In fact, due to an increase in the costs of the necessary material, the houses built under Law 178/76 were completed with a considerable contribution from the owners, sometimes forced to sell some plots of land. While all those homes built in more recent times and possibly belonging to many non-resident families benefited from the evolution of the legislation.

XXVII - THE NEW POGGIOREALE

The new Poggioreale is located in the area of the old farmhouse of Mandria di Mezzo, in an area of more than 40 hectares of hilly land that slopes south down to within a few hundred meters of the Belice River, with the housing units extending southwest along the road named Viale del Belice. This enters the provincial road to Salaparuta, Partanna, S. Margherita Belice, Montevago and so on.

The connection with the Palermo-Sciacca expressway is through a well-maintained section of road recently lined with trees and illuminated up to the "Valle del Belice" cooperative winery, the first and only cooperative established in Poggioreale in the 1970s for the storage of grapes, produced above all by our vineyards.

The road connecting to the expressway ends with a roundabout, in the center of which stands a wonderful ornamental palm that adds a touch of grace to the town's entrance.

The visitor who instead reaches the town from the expressway on the outskirts has the pleasure of reaching a large square with architectural works of great value that represent the business card of the new Municipality: Piazza Elìm in neoclassical style, which reproduces the ancient Agorà, destined to become the town's meeting place like in the old town, and its center of life. It is an imposing structure that strikes visitors for its artistically worked colonnades enriched by two caryatids on the left side and two in the upper colonnade, the work of the Florentine sculptor Paolo Borghi, for the harmonious and stylistically appealing movements because they briefly immerse you in the center of an ancient civilization, that of the Greeks; a civilization that has been fascinating since our first studies of it in school. It is the work of the famous architect Paolo Portoghesi (see photo no. 37).

Adjacent to the square and in front of those who enter the town stands the clock that rises triumphantly from Town Hall and strikes the eye with its front façade featuring a semicircular structure with the coat of arms of the Municipality in the middle. On the right side of the square is the chapel of St. Anthony of Padua, the patron saint of Poggioreale, the work of the architect Franco Purini; the municipal theater designed by the architect L. Giocondo is on the northeast side along with the library and the ethnoanthropological

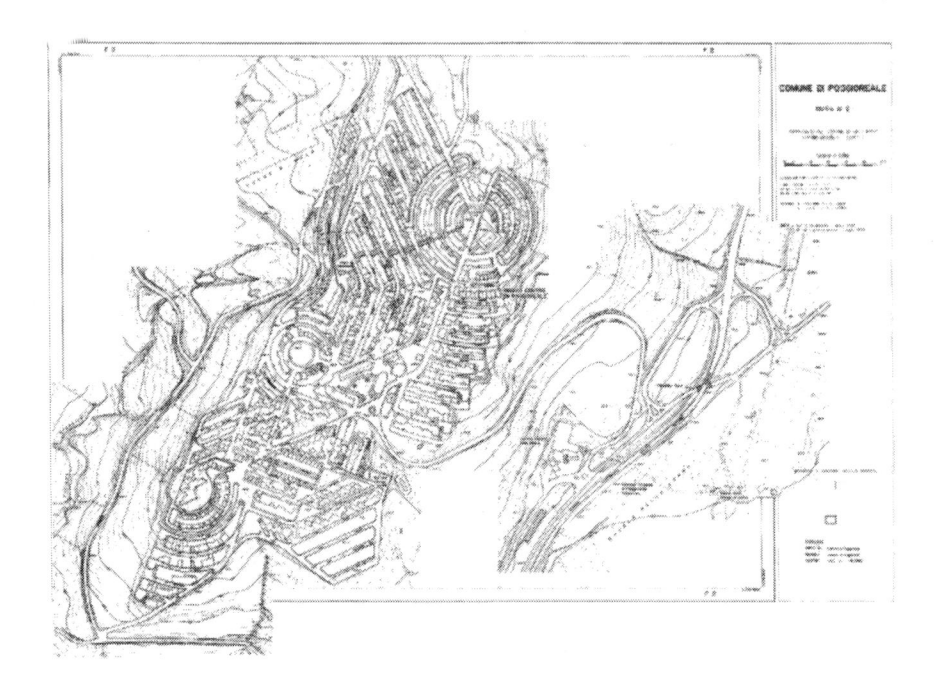

Photo 36 - Planimetry of the new town

museum which is quite interesting because it collects the remains of the peasant civilization that have since passed on to become history, but always alive and symbolizing the tenacity, the courage, the spiritual and moral strength of our fathers who in the hard and exhausting work of the past had tempered the soul and the body to challenge poor weather and the adversities of life. The municipal swimming pool is to the south of the square, an equally imposing work by the architect P. Portoghesi, but it remained incomplete and exposed to the slaughter of strangers who had recently tried to break down its doors and windows; to the north of the Town Hall there is another work by the architect Purini, the bus station, in short all monuments of a very welcoming business card.

The articulation then of well cared for streets, enlivened by the presence of trees that flank them and embellish them, the frequent clearings that open between the intersections of the streets, also graced by interesting housing units for the movement of elevations and structural shapes similar to extensive villas, inviting inhabitants to enjoy their time there: I believe that all these elements give the visitor the full and right feeling that living in a village like ours, a real jewel in the face of the angry cities of our time which consume you day after day for the stressful life that is led there, for the poisoned air that enters the lungs, for the formidable traffic that unnerves the fibers of the brain and heart, should be seen as a privilege, like that of the souls who long for the peace of paradise, instead of the fires of hell.

The expression of a well-known and famous German poet and writer Johann W. Goethe, who visited some villages on the Amalfi coast in Italy in the years between 1786- 1788, was so astonished that when speaking to some local people, he said: "When you are in Heaven, you will say: well, the usual life!" Those he was speaking to would ask "Why do you say this?" and he responded, "Because you have heaven here." With this I do not want to exaggerate the amenities of our village, considering it a paradise on earth and, so much so that the comparison with the Amalfi coast does not hold, I provide it merely as an association of ideas to emphasize instead the other comparison between the chaotic life of the city and the serenity that is sensed in a small community with an agricultural economy, where there is no lack of conditions to satisfy the demands of life, not contained within the limits of the indispensable.

Meanwhile, the town enjoys many other requirements, has all the useful services for a civil and modern life: there is adequate health care during the day by the family doctors, Dr. Salvaggio and Dr. Drago who divide the patients; at night from 8 p.m. to 8. a.m. we have the doctors of the medical guard who alternate their services. Should there be a need for emergency hospitalization,

Photo 37 - Piazza Elimo in the new town

there is an ambulance available which is based in the nearby Salaparuta, with which the equipped hospitals can be reached in little time thanks to the good connections of the town with the nearby cities of Castelvetrano, Sciacca, and even Palermo. There is a health officer, a function performed today by Dr. Rosario Vella and a veterinarian, Dr. Leonardo Strada, who are responsible for the sanitation services and medical assistance for sheep and cattle farms in our area, respectively.

Also worthy of note are the very well-stocked and welcoming bakeries, the supermarkets that carry everything, the ovens with good local bread, the bus service for taking students to kindergarten and elementary school, home care for the elderly who are alone and in need of moral aid, and the collaboration of young assistants for essential services, the sports facilities for youth who have a soccer field in the area to the southwest of the town, a recently built five-a-side soccer field with particular details, and finally the same site of the town is easily connected with the coast and the seaside resorts (Porto Palo, Fiore beach, Selinunte...), with the larger cities for shopping and the distractions that cannot be found locally. These are all privileges that would give the impression of a flourishing town rich in social life, in a spirit of solidarity, where the human contact of the time when you were once poor, but fraternal by the continuous meetings and breath of neighbors, had maintained and found much more intense forms of cohesion than in the past.

Instead, the reflections of today's civilization of technology, progress, more or less sophisticated machines, electronics, rapid communications, have spread through our youth faster than in certain more internal towns not affected by the earthquake, almost extinguishing habits and traditions that are dragged on today unenthusiastically and without heartfelt participation, perhaps to satisfy the nostalgic memories of that segment of the population that has left their heart in the old village.

Yet among the activities planned and carried out by the administrations that have succeeded each other since the 1980s, after the transfer of the population to the new urban center, it is clear that the incentives for the resumption of traditional festivals have not been neglected, indeed they have been complemented by many other initiatives at the recreational-cultural level. The introduction of Poggioreale week falling on the anniversary of the fair that took place on August 24-25 has given the citizens the opportunity to enjoy various cultural events every year, entertainment that includes theatrical performances, film screenings, folkloristic shows, light music with the participation of

Photo 38 - townhall building with tower

nationally famous singers. The Municipality of Poggioreale was the first among the Municipalities of the Belice Valley to establish the week of cultural initiatives. Other occasions for meeting are the festivals of ricotta and wine, the exhibition of the cheeses of the Valley now in its seventh edition, the provincial selections of the national competition of Miss Italia in the prestigious Piazza Elimo, the competition in recent years for the national prize of poetry and narrative, a literary/poetic event that has brought prestigious personalities to our village for the award. The presence of the famous director Giuseppe Tornatore, who twice chose the old town to make two films, Malèna and L'uomo delle stelle (The Star Maker) is also particularly remembered. Finally, Poggioreale was the protagonist of two documentaries broadcast by Rai Tre, the first dedicated to the old town and the second to the new.

    A rich series of events aimed at promoting human and cultural growth, encouraging meetings between families, friends, and relatives to enjoy a pleasant and relaxing evening full of the sense of well-being that human relationships, lived in the dimension of reciprocal and sincere pleasure, can give to the daily life of the whole community.

    In his role as organizer and sometimes as conductor of these activities, I turned to Dr. Mario Pace to ask him if these events also extended to break down the wall of silence and solitude in which people live in the long periods interconnected between one event and the other, creating an occasion for anticipated and heartfelt participation. He replied: "With the transfer of the population to the new town which took place at the beginning of the 1980s, there was a period of social, cultural, and recreational dynamism, perhaps as a continuity of the very long period lived in the slums; a period that lasted until the nineties. Since then, an ever-increasing decline has begun. Now the human relations are constantly deteriorating and in any case lack the necessary warmth."

    In a survey conducted by the journalist Dino Chiara, published together with some photographs of the old and new towns by Mauro D'Agati, in the monthly magazine D distributed with the newspaper La Repubblica of 10/31/2000, it read: "... the real ghost town, the one stunned by an unreal silence, misunderstood by the inhabitants themselves, spectral because it has no places for aggregation and historical memory, is the ultra-modern one where the population was transferred en masse in the early 1980s." The statement seems somewhat exaggerated, even if there is a touch of truth, because more than 20 years after the transfer of the inhabitants, entering the town at certain times of the day, one gets the impression of entering a town where silence dominates the streets, in houses with locked doors and windows that would seem to be uninhabited, if the presence of some car did not contradict this impression.

The demographic decline has gradually reduced the population's size from the year of the earthquake to the present day.

So we ask ourselves: what are the reasons for this exodus of young people and families to other regions? And why did the Poggiorealese not reconstitute the meeting points in the new town as in the destroyed one?

To answer these questions, I believe that we must briefly analyze the historical courses that have changed the cultural, economic, and social path of the earthquake victims in the phases of transition from the old town to the barracks and from the barracks these to the total transfer to the new Poggioreale.

The spirit of adaptation to life in the slums has already been mentioned which, despite certain complaints founded in the desire for a comfortable home, had restored the balance of daily life between families at work, relationship with the environment and with people, a menage of life reconstituted on the traces of a past that still seemed to stand on the load-bearing skeleton of a seemingly solid civilization, but in fact undermined and eroded by obvious manifestations of life which were changed and emerging from the serene confrontation between two very close generations: fathers and children. On the subject of life in the barracks, I had spoken of a convergence-divergence without impact, two antithetical ages had been marked by a soft and gradual passage confused among other things by the respectful attitude of the children towards their fathers, the result of an education built on certain memories of the not-so-distant patriarchal family.

However, the population of the barracks included children, youth in their first years of school, those born in the same slums that had no roots in the old town.

I would also like to state that while in the slums, the contacts with the old town were very frequent and this muffled the emotional discomfort. Given this premise, I think it is indicative to point out that in the 1980s the families, with the exception of some who remained in the barracks for some time, possibly because their new home was not yet finished, moved into the houses of the new town, prompted by the violence of the wind that had uncovered and damaged many of the barracks. Here they had the privilege of living in apartments with all the comforts of a civil house: a rational division of rooms, possibly with two bathrooms equipped with quality sanitary fittings and complete with a shower and bathtub; an electric bell or intercom and no longer the doors of the past in which doors were merely a privilege of a few families; indeed, they were walnut or mahogany doors of simple or fine workmanship; an electrical system for opening the entrance door to the apartment instead of a cord connected with the bolt of a lock; the installation of a telephone in all the homes; marble or tile floors; the exposure and brightness of the rooms already foreseen in the design of the building lots that ran in a line between the road, overlooking the land intended for flowers and gardens and the entrance to the garage and pedestrian area from which the entrance to the apartments is accessed.

And with the allocation of more substantial sums in the last days of the reconstruction, very finely finished and, I would say, stately homes were built.

The satisfaction of the families who took up residence in such welcoming accommodations was clear in their eyes; in little time they adequately furnished their living rooms and other rooms with decent or even expensive furniture depending on their availability.

The inhabitants of Poggioreale had finally been gratified with lodgings that compensated for the vicissitudes of the earthquake, but also the centuries-old discomforts of living, at least for a high percentage of the families, in narrow and battered huts or in dilapidated apartments among the smells of straw and hay mixed with the dung and piss of animals rising from the barn below or adjacent to the living quarters. Taking advantage of a used and abused expression, I believe they passed from the stables to the stars.

But the satisfaction for such a beautiful house did not correspond to the mood of the most extensive segment of the adult population that had been uprooted from the environment in which they had deeply sunk their roots and was then transplanted into an unfamiliar housing context devoid of "historical memory," that is, the memory of all those small and large things that create and develop the overall set of the existence of man: the streets, the squares, the recreational and social circles, the multitude of voices and known passages, the meetings, the exchange of ideas and opinions, the deafening noise of the gutters emptying rainwater onto the streets full of rounded cobblestones and cleaned by the wash that descended to the valley to swell the drainage of waters in the valley and in that of the Capuchin convent, flowing first towards the Cusumano area to then flow into the Belice River and the other in the parallel channel to join the valley with the first. A whole world of subjects and objects that fervently move around every human being, penetrating into our being, give a voice to consciousness and characterize the personality that grows and develops in a relationship of emotional balance, locked by memory. Memory is what remains, because nothing can take it away, not even time. In fact, it is the only good that remains between the continuous and relentless setting of ages and the succession of others that develop and evolve from the first.

If in the structure of the new housing center the characteristics of the old were not minimally respected, which would not only have made the transfer

Photo 39 - Front facade - Town Hall

of the people less traumatic, but also would have allowed a slow and gradual recovery of the socio-cultural habits essential for everyday life without psychological repercussions. Hence it is not difficult to imagine the reasons for the state of gradual isolation of the people from when they began to live in the new homes.

In fact, I believe the disconnect between the old and the new town is due to the urban structure of the new, projected into the distant future and based on projects of a hopeful future of the community of Poggioreale: the various voices and promises that were shouted out to the four winds on the economic renaissance in the immediate aftermath of the earthquake thanks to the presumptuous interventions of the State, which promised an impressive new life in those towns that had been shamefully and most dismally abandoned for centuries, perhaps fueled the illusion of the competent bodies and the same architects who deluded themselves in conceiving a futuristic structure suitable to accommodate very intense commercial and industrial traffic, as if they were convinced that the future expansion of the town could compete with the chaotic cities of our time.

May the hope inherent in the design of the urban structure find concrete expression in the social and civil reality of our fellow citizens in the near future. But this wish does not preclude, at the present time, the possibility of considering that the pedestrian and drivable roads, the arrangement of the lots that envisaged the construction of the houses with a prospectus entering that of the next house, all favored the dispersion of human contacts, as if everything had been devised to prevent the woman of one house from talking with the neighbor of the next.

Even the location of the Mother Church in a peripheral hill of the perimeter layout of the town seems to have been an unthoughtful choice, nor suggested by the intention of facilitating the access of the Parish inhabitants in the opposite peripheral areas, whose distances did not allow people of a certain age to participate in the celebration of Holy Mass, if there is no good soul that accompanies them with a car. The lack of evaluation of the problem and a hint of irony leads us to say that it is, however, compensated by the construction of an imposing bridge, on majestic columns, which should have connected the Church with a staircase, which is introduced between the houses of the almost central area of the town. If I am not mistaken, I think it was a scandalous waste of capital for an imposingly useless operation, which then gave rise to several controversies spread by the press of the time.

As a result, the frequency of parishioners in the church has thinned, also due to the thinning of the religious fervor of the past. With this I am not seeking to affirm that the villagers have become atheists; the living sense of religiosity is always there. On Sunday the Church is almost always full; St. Anthony of Padua, patron saint of the town, always receives a moving devotion, but the intensity of the religious spirit seems to be more limited than in the past.

The comparison of the present with the religiosity of the past is compatibly risky, because each era is characterized by different customs, changing values, life models suggested by phases of economic development which are very different from other eras that time has given to the past, movements of thought that lead to the acquisition of a new mentality and new styles of behavior. Consider, for example, that in the old town there were many churches: the Mother Church, a work of Baroque style built in 1647 whose altar was surmounted by the Heart of Jesus; the Oratory annexed to the Mother Church, where the urn of dead Christ was kept; the Church of the Holy Souls in Piazza Elimo; the Church of St. Anthony in the main street protected by iron gates; the Church of Jesus and Mary located in the clearing of the ancient Castle; the Church of Our Lady of Sorrows with the simulacrum of Our Lady in the central crypt; the chapel of the Immaculate Conception adjacent to the hospital; the little church of the Capuchin Fathers with an interesting reliquary that adorned the apse and above all with its wooden Crucifix of great artistic value, which today dominates the front wall of the High Altar of the current Mother Church. And as if that were not enough, there was also the chapel of the Madonna del Rosario, commonly identified as the church of Tagliavia three kilometers from the town, and finally the chapel of the former Cautalì feud founded by Don Pietro Cangiatosi for the *borgesi* and their families. There were many priests who worked in the environment, who gave confidence to the people, who organized meetings with the boys at the headquarters of Azione Cattolica to sensitize them to faith and love.

Today for religious ceremonies, the faithful count on only one minister of God, Rev. Arch. Don Giuseppe La Rocca, the IX Archpriest from the religious autonomy of the old Parish, after his predecessors: Rev. Arch. Nicola Scardino, Rev. Arch. Giuseppe Giurlanda, Rev. Arch. Vincenzo Caronna, Rev. Arch. Vincenzo Agosta, Rev. Arch. Vincenzo Caronna, Rev. Arch. Girolamo Gulino, Rev. Arch. Dr. Nunzio Caronna, Rev. Arch. Girolamo Corte.

Therefore, if the fact that the comparison apparently reveals two very distinct and different eras, this does not mean that one can consider it either a sign of the faded religious sensitivity, or of a phenomenon of adaptation to the circumstances. In any case, it is certain that in the religious sense of life it is the support of the moral balance and the strength to overcome the difficulties of which the journey of man is often dotted.

If, after this parenthesis on the religiosity of the Poggiorealese, we consider the large spaces and the large squares scattered between roads with a semicircular pattern, almost making it more difficult to acquire the development dynamics of the road network and the layout of the housing units, we are not surprised by the considerable acclimatization difficulties of the fellow citizens.

I therefore believe that the urban structure of the new town is the first cause justifying the widespread and generalized observation of a spectral ghost town immersed in the silence and solitude of the streets. This is not to argue that the new town had to be inspired by a typically medieval structure with roads converging in the middle of the town, where the Town Hall, Mother Church, the main square with the presence of bars, social and recreational circles, seats of political parties and main shops would have been located, nor a structure compressed in a few hectares of land as the old town.

It would have been absurd for an urban structure to be static in the face of a society galloping towards development goals that give, I repeat, a new face to the values of life, to daily habits, to social relations, and to the needs of the people.

However, if on the other hand in these phases of transition we had tried to reconcile the old and new in tune with what had occurred on the level of ideas and mentality between fathers and children, the traumatic deprivation of human and social relationships would have been less incisive in blocking initiatives which, although not finding in the new and different town the conditions for a restoration of the old lifestyle, would have reestablished a relationship with the environment which was gentler and more open to forms of aggregation.

It could be objected that the construction of a town destined to challenge the centuries does not have the character of precariousness as the life of a man, therefore it cannot respect a passage as soft as that interconnected between two generations; but neither is it an expression of human sensitivity to erase a more or less long period of his existence from a man's life.

All the middle-aged people, man or woman, have left their hearts there in the old town, the best part of themselves, that for which they haven't been able to regain ownership in the new. In the first months of her transfer to a working-class house, the mother wrote to her distant son a few days before closing her eyes to life: "Beloved son, here in the new town I suffer the anguish of loneliness. I am an old woman and I do not go out in the streets; it seems to me that I am in hell: I never talk to anyone, I do not see anyone passing by, not even my cousin who came to see me in the barracks a hundred times, now she does not come anymore, we are very far away. I send you hugs, your mother who cannot wait for the moment to see you again." But her son never saw her again.

Photo 40 - Community theater

These nostalgic feelings for the destroyed town are still alive after more than 20 years; in fact, from a survey of samples of elderly people, there is now talk of deportation in these barracks in the most dismal isolation: "... it is as if they had torn our heart from our chest and our person had split: the heart lays there between the ruins and the body, deprived of feelings, is here." The case of one woman who never adapted should be recalled, with her mind assiduously turned to her ancient home until she manifested signs of such a possessive memory that she lived the rest of her long life with the illusion of being in the house where her children were born and where she had spent a happy life as a wife and mother.

Therefore, the urban structure of the new town was one of the causes of the lack of amalgamation of the inhabitants of Poggioreale, but it is not the only motivation because there were many other collateral factors. An urban layout on an area of more than 40 hectares of land that accommodates only 1,800 inhabitants, while it could be home to 6,000, can only appear to the eyes of those who love it as a town teeming with people, crowding the streets to go shopping or for other family tasks: ours is a small village with an agricultural economy and is not a commercial or industrial center. Furthermore, we must not underestimate the presence in every house of one or more television sets that I consider a very interesting and at the same time disruptive instrument of information and distraction and not only for families in the neighborhood, but also among the same members of a family.

Television addiction is very widespread today and draws the attention of people to the point that the interest in following any program, whether good or not, compensates the need to communicate and the natural sense of friendship.

If we then consider the other segment of the population, that of young people, that is, those born in the barracks or who moved there at a young age and those born in the new Poggioreale, I think it is appropriate to bear in mind that these same children have lost, within the global perspective of their formative processes, the fragile customs attached to the culture of their fathers, especially in the new town where the continuity of traditional life systems has been broken. Not having local models to inspire them, they followed the natural course of evolution of the times without the braking action of the past, as we could see in the small urban towns of interior Sicily that had not been affected by the earthquake. The life project of the mass media prevailed, however always contained within the limits of a small environment and with a purely agricultural economy.

Another phenomenon that must be noted, in my opinion, is the need for parents to urge their children to continue their studies so that they do not remain in the margins of a society that relentlessly runs to gain economic and unrealistic privileges, where bureaucratic barriers are fed by savage and complicated legislation that confuses the course of things, rather than streamlining it.

Thus school and education are the essential prerequisites for the integration of young people into the complex society of our time; the simplest work activities are regulated by complicated bureaucratic scaffolding, by a legislative system that is so complex that it is necessary to turn to professionals to complete bureaucratic processes that protect the rights and duties of the citizen. Having obtained a diploma or a degree, and not finding the possibility of exercising the profession in his local environment, the young person seeks work outside and possibly adapts to work with a fixed salary, even if this is not congruent with the degree obtained.

In some respects, young students do not have solid roots in their environment, except for the bond with their family. They travel daily to attend high schools in nearby cities such as Castelvetrano, Alcamo, Sciacca, Palermo, cities that offer, among other things, living spaces and distractions more suited to their age and the conquered freedom of relations between boys and girls. So the town of origin could offer the distractions of their fathers when the meetings were spontaneous and unplanned, when they were active in the square or in social circles, there were friends of the same age and the older people with whom they exchanged opinions, and there was a fear of the experience that others had gained in a longer and perhaps more suffered experience. Free time then found pleasant space in these spontaneous, sincere, and relaxing encounters. Today the new generations consider these distractions absurd, with the flavor of a primitive and archaic mental structure. Modern needs are suggested by the life models that the press and above all television propose and impose on the most naive and fertile age groups, so much so that it is enough to throw a seed, which immediately puts roots and sprouts.

Hence the phenomenon of conformism of dress, of the manifestations of behavior, of language, and of a pseudo individualism that on the one hand is betrayed in conforming to the models of other young people up to the loss of individuality, and on the other stiffens with the detachment from the past and from the generations that were and are part of it. These are aspects of an emerging cosmopolitan trend that is spreading into forms of larvae even in our small socio-cultural environments.

If the diagnosis of young people's current relationship with their environment is based on truth, it is not difficult to deduce that the exodus and the consequent demographic decline of the town is undoubtedly due to the lack of employment resources, which are the backbone, but the other reasons including contacts with the larger cities that young people have today, for reasons of study or to find distractions that their town does not offer, are transformed into bonds that favor the predisposition towards future life choices of a wider scope. It is true that this predisposition is rightly supported by a state of force majeure, but it is also true that it precludes the spirit of initiative of young people to create employment resources in their own environment by intensifying and developing existing structures in terms of expansion, and exploiting both their cultural training for a conscious management of their actions, and certain incentives for establishing autonomous companies.

The real problem is also in the forms of welfare in national and European policy that extinguish new initiatives to be exploited among the children of current agricultural entrepreneurs; it thus happens that a graduate in agriculture prefers to find employment in a public body with a modest monthly salary instead of joining their father's company with the prospect of exploiting it with different and specialized crops according to market demands.

The mechanization of agricultural work has changed the work-employment ratio. Today sharecropping, leasing, and running *gabelli* in the local area no longer exist and the land is divided into small or large companies and cultivated directly by the same owners thanks to the very sophisticated mechanical means that allow them to grow specialized and extensive crops throughout the company's smaller or larger areas and using the help of machines owned by "third parties." The main crops are the vineyards that provide the most profitable production of the estate; then the cultivation of melons and watermelons is very widespread, whose yield in the years in which the market is not saturated exceeds that of the vineyards; finally, the extensive cultivation of wheat takes place, whose production costs in terms of time and employment are less onerous than other crops and with an irrelevant yield if it were not for the integration that the European Community provides in the form of a contribution for each hectare of land cultivated with wheat.

So the economy of the Poggiorealese population, which is predominantly agricultural, is profitable and supports the few commercial activities existing in the town with an adequate yield. It is therefore obvious that where machines replace human arms they create unemployment for the working class; in Poggioreale, especially after the reconstruction of the town which had given work not only to our fellow citizens but also to masons, carpenters, plasterers from areas not affected by the earthquake, there was a phenomenon of unemployment for the working class which could not find continuous work, also in consideration of the increased needs of life, which emigrated and continues to emigrate to Northern Italy where they will be able to carry out more remunerative and safer projects for themselves and their families.

An examination of the population movements of Poggiorealese from 1958 to 2001 shows that the population of 3,000 inhabitants in 1958 gradually thinned down to 1,723 (last census of 10/20/2001) with a decrease of 1,274 people. In 43 years, 3,455 inhabitants and 2,090 immigrants have emigrated, with an annual average of 82 emigrants and 49 immigrants. A bitter observation that leaves us very perplexed about the future fate of our homeland.

It is true that the above figures show a gradual decrease in births in line with the data established at national and, I would say, European level, but it is also true that the phenomenon of migration in 40 years does not register any phases of arrest, even in the most intense decade of the town's reconstruction. This data raises concerns and leads to hypotheses, perhaps absurd and meaningless, on the use of remedies, an intervention policy that prepares the tools for the information and preparation of young people to find work resources in their own environment, to profit on initiatives that open the doors to occupational activities that require culture, investment, professional specificity, given by special schools in the field of industry, trade, the manufacture of the products of the earth.

We must free ourselves of the exasperated individualism that isolates and does not bring us together, creating discredit on initiatives regardless of where they come from; we must encourage associationism, listen with great humility to what the experience of others provides us to enrich what we do have; we must ponder and rationalize the goals that we set out to achieve in order to avoid letting ourselves be carried away by the frenzied rush of the most exasperated society of our time that runs without brakes and without balance, with obvious signs of the loss of the human and social aspects that so occupies our nature as men.

Unfortunately, we often stifle this sense of the human that is within and is part of us because the mass media, the greed for money, the freedom to satisfy the pleasures of life not supported by values, the insane criterion of interpreting the freedom to use and consume the interests of others to the detriment of the interests and rights of others, we stun and run and we no longer cultivate friendship, social relationships, that ever-so-soothing and necessary relationship to measure ourselves with others with sincerity and receive the great benefit of feeling not like a robot, but a person who comes to fruition with balanced common sense in everyday life.

The choice of studies for young people should be aimed at achieving professional skills suitable for promoting work initiatives in the area and for those who consider that they will find employment opportunities in implementing these initiatives.

In 1914, Archpriest Dr. Nunzio Caronna in the book: *L'Arch. Caronna al suo popolo* (Arch. Caronna to his people) spoke to the Poggiorealese in Piazza Elimo, inviting them to fight to obtain the division of the Cautali Grande feud, a measure he considered essential so that farmers could rise from their current state of poverty and misery. In this book we read: "... families cry on the brink of financial abyss, the land has become not their own for a set of known and unknown causes, the arms are not enough to provide for consumption, the capital is lacking, America swallows the most skilled workers and in addition to education, we lack work and bread". Then he asks: "And why do the great shareholders not show themselves here, generous to throw valid capital into the field, to give growth to industries, factories, exploiting the infinite energies that the land and the waters of the Belice provide us? And why are there not also emission institutes, artistic and agricultural companies, mechanical laboratories, where we can obtain work and bread for all, for all in this land?" Immediately afterwards Caronna adds: "But I banish industrial and commercial whims for a plague that is only beautiful for nature's poetry, and instead is poor in resources, large capital, commercial topics!" But today, a century or so later, things have changed and preparing young people to establish their place locally is not a whim, it is a prospect that can be carried out in a longer or shorter period of time, exploiting the governmental and European measures that encourage programs of this kind.

I think it is appropriate to dismantle the mentality that is quite common in Sicily of a fixed job, and the other even more absurd and now outdated mentality of quite some time that a young person with a degree is not advised to deal with the countryside and specialized crops. I ask, would it be so degrading?

And this is a mentality typical of those who do not see beyond the tip of their own nose. Culture and agriculture are an inseparable combination if you want to keep up with the times. And the mentality of savings in the form of "bricks" must also be eradicated, another attitude inhibiting the tendency to invest to expand, increase profits for the benefit of oneself and local workers. It seems to me that the time has come to embark on new paths; it is time to say no to degrees, to diplomas which in an oversaturated climate do not provide an opportunity for work and force young people to suffer the humiliation of long years of waiting before finding a solution or a place of refuge, possibly choosing the routes of the widespread malpractice of political customers and other forms of depressing exploitation of the recommendation, except evidently for young people who stand out for their excellent performance in studies who must not resort to the tortuous ways of a corrupt society.

The renaissance of the Belìce Valley so desired by the administrations of the various municipalities affected by the earthquake, so hoped for by members of the press and politicians affected by the emotion of the moment in those days of disaster and dramatic circumstance has not arrived 33 years after the earthquake, but has provided politicians with the opportunistic chance to use an always touching argument to add hot incisiveness and vibrant vigor to the rallies of the square. And the problem, wandering from one occasion to another, from one event to another, from one electoral campaign to another, has been permanently lost between the words, the ups and downs, the allusions, the controversies, so much so that it is no longer found. However, the responsibility is not to be attributed only to the political bodies with unfulfilled promises: I believe a part of the responsibility should be borne by the people of the earthquake-stricken towns who, accustomed to delegating to the other institutions, always wait for the manna to fall from heaven.

The solicitations must start from the bottom, the programs must be proposed, presented, and brought to the attention of the bodies in charge with detail by the populations concerned, united by the intention of pursuing common interests and common goals.

These are considerations that are likely to be interpreted as empty rhetoric and unfounded suggestions addressed to the young Poggiorealese, suggestions given by those who look at the problems from the outside and with the presumption of competence, when in fact the reality is quite different, especially for those who have directly experienced it. However, many years spent in contact with young people have left me with a professional distortion, that of illuding myself of having given them something useful for their future lives, transforming the lessons on the various authors of Italian literature into life lessons, because I was convinced that it was my duty to inform the young, to instruct them and prepare them for life, to help them grow, to think about the various problems the authors presented, updating them with the intention of promoting and developing the processes of internalization, reflection and critical evaluation.

A job that gratified me; as I said, perhaps it was an illusion; as Foscolo wrote, "But what does it matter that it is an illusion, if it helps us live life." And since historical-social news assumes value not so much for the people who have personally lived the facts, but for the youth who do not know their past and for all the future generations to whom the invitation to maintain the prestige of their town of origin must be addressed: this is and will be an act of respect for our ancestors who lived and perished on this land.

But the most striking gesture that the young Poggiorealese can express, along with the municipal administrations as a sign of love for their roots and the rediscovery of their identity, will be the commitment to return the center of the historic town to their fellow citizens. Preserving the memory of the past through the functional recovery and consolidation of works in the historic town is the most tangible sign of the attachment of present and future generations to the memory of the others who once were, whose life was lived among hardships and hopes, between the love for one's family and the tenacity of the work, between the interweaving of spiritual serenity and the spiritual composure dictated by the balance of daily life, between thoughtfulness and wisdom suggested by the culture, the fruit of the experience of their parents. This is and will be an inexhaustible source of inalienable and perennial values to draw from to establish the future of our homeland and raise its name in the
disintegration of today's society.

In this regard and in support of these last reflections, I would like to quote a book entitled *Randagio, il figlio del secolo* (Stray, the child of a century) written by a Poggiorealese, Prof. Gigi Cangelosi, who as a young man was the protagonist of cultural activities in our town and the author of several publications of poems and other texts. The book narrates the story of a man, Claudio, as a symbol of fleeting time, who because of the increasing scarcity of humanity has become a stray, who confronts himself, feels his distant origins as a man who "has become lost in the dark meanders of existential grayness."

In the detachment of man from his origins, the author sees the rarefaction of the human, the beginning of the conflict between the man of before and that of today who has lost his identity.

As mentioned, the recovery project can be said to have started. The consolidation of the Agosta house, intended as a museum of archaeological finds of the Castellaccio area, was carried out by the administration of the former Mayor Gaetano Selvaggio. The plan was then supported by the subsequent administration of Mayor Caterina Tusa, whose arrival included the recovery of some sites of the urban context of the historic center of Poggioreale in the three-year plan of 1998-2000. This plan has also been considered by the current administration, although I am aware of the insensitivity of the political bodies responsible for its financing because it was considered not aimed at the concept of investment-yield and employment.

The young Poggiorealese have the privilege of being raised among the affections of healthy families, not entrusted from an early age to institutions as happens to many children whose parents, unfortunately both occupied with work for the entire day, have very little dialogue with their children. They try to fill this void with gifts and an abundance of the things that they desire and that they do not desire, but do not give what they would actually need: the warmth and affection of the mother for an effective sensitization to the feeling of love. Those who do not receive love cannot give it, growing with a hardened soul, insensitive to the spirit of solidarity towards thy neighbor. Those who are accustomed to receiving things before even desiring them do not feel any satisfaction, nor do they grow with the awareness that the taste of life arises from the struggle to overcome the difficulties encountered, to achieve the goals that each of us aims to achieve. If this continuous urging of will is lacking, there is a risk of living daily life with apathy and to fight it, emotion is sought in transgressions.

This healthy social plague can then find support in respect for the traditions of our ancestors, who with their customs based on simple, modest, crude life systems, but not polluted by sophisticated, sometimes excessive and uncontrolled attitudes, point to a benchmark every time, which is the balance of family life and relationships that show signs of faltering.

In an article of *Giornale di Sicilia* of December 10, 2002, the journalist Cristiano Del Riccio writes that, according to a project by American scholars specializing in "positive psychology," the secret of happiness is in knowing how to appreciate the joys of family and in surrounding oneself with friends; it is very beneficial to not give importance to money. "Materialism is the poison of happiness," argues the psychologist Ed. Diener from the University of Illinois.

"The most satisfied people are those who are able to immerse themselves in what they are doing and forget the passage of time," says psychologist Mihaly Csihszent of Claremont University. In short, the recipe is: many friends, enjoy daily activities, no envy, know how to forgive. "Money doesn't count, but friends, family, knowing how to enjoy the small things."

If these solicitations to a more serene, less pressing, and quieter life interpret an elusive tendency of the most industrialized populations to blame fatigue and prefer a more sober and moderate life, then our past points us to examples that we must preserve very protectively and with a spirit of humility.

In a conference whose theme was precisely the recovery and consolidation plan of the works of our town that had not been completely razed to the ground nor reduced to a pile of rubble, the Architect Prof. Paolo Portoghesi introduces his speech with the following words, which in 1859 a tribal leader had addressed to the governor of the state of Washington with deep feeling: "Every corner of this country is sacred to my people for some memory, some sad experience; even the rocks that seem insensitive, when silent sweat sumptuously under the sun, vibrating the memory of past events of my tribe.

Even the dust on which we walk gladly accepts our feet, because it is the ashes of our ancestors, and our feet know that the ground is happy to support us, because it is rich in the life of our ancestors."

I could also add that in presenting my book in the main hall of the *Galileo Galilei Scientific High School,* I also thanked all those present and the scholars who had presented it, and said: "Lastly, I reserve a special thanks that I address with my heart in hand to the Mayor of the Municipality of Poggioreale and to the friends and relatives who came to bring the presence of my dear and beloved town here, destroyed by the earthquake of 1968. When I say dear and beloved town, I know that I am using a cliché; but clichés are good, because in those ruins left abandoned and in silence, in those ruins exposed to bad weather and the wear and tear of the infallible forces of time which destroy and erase everything, the most dear memories of my life are carved with indelible blows of a chisel, the memories of childhood that bind my life to its origins, to which I look with deep feeling." I lastly concluded with a quote by Ernesto Di Martino that I found included in the introduction to the book of poems in Sicilian dialect by Prof. Mario Grasso, literary director of the publishing house "Prova d'Autore." For the specific relevance with the reflections made previously, I think it is appropriate to close with the same passage of Di Martino which reads: "Those who do not have roots, who are cosmopolitan, move towards the death of passion and the human: in order not to be provincial it is necessary to have a village living in memory, to which the image and the heart always return again and which the work of science and poetry reshapes in a universal voice."

BIBLIOGRAPHY

AA.VV., *1968 - Terremoto in Sicilia,* Ed . Andò, Palermo, 1968.

Giuseppe Bonetta, *L'istruzione elementare nella Sicilia dell '800,* Ed. Sellerio, Palermo, 1981.

Gesualdo Bufalino - Nunzio Zago, *Cento Sicilie: testimonianza di un ritratto,* Ed. Nuova Italia, Florence, 1993.

Arch. N. Caronna, *Memorie storiche di Poggioreale,* Ed. Tipografia Pontificia, Palermo, 1901.

Arch. N. Caronna, *Vita civile di Poggioreale,* Tip. Pontificia, Palermo, 1906.
Arch. N. Caronna, *L'Arch. Caronna al suo popolo,* Ed. Giuseppe Gianfala, Palermo, 1914.

Can. Dr. Arch. N. Caronna, *Discorsi vari,* Ed. Libreria dell'Oratorio, Palermo.

G. Cangialosi, *Randagio. il figlio del secolo,* Ed. Tip. E. Ariani, Florence, 1992.

G. Cocchiera, *Il folklore siciliano nel Museo Pitrè ,* Ist. di Storia delle tradizioni popolari, Palermo.

Santi Correnti, *La Sicilia del Seicento,* Ed. Newton Compton, Rome, 1995.

Salvatore Costanzo, *I giorni di Ghibellina,* Ed. Flaccovio, Palermo.

S. Di Benedetto, *La Sicilia non è un 'isola,* Ed . Ila Palma, Palermo.

S. Di Benedetto, *Civiltà contadina,* Ed. De Donato, Palermo.

V. Di Giovanni, *Effemeridi siciliane,* Palermo.

Fazzello Tommaso, *Storia della Sicilia,* Palermo, 1832.

G. A. Garufi, *Patti agrari e comuni di nuova istituzione in Sicilia.*

B. Graffanino, *Salaparuta, ieri e oggi,* Tip. Fiamma Serafica, Palermo, 1975.

Leonardo Lo Presti, *Genealogia della famiglia Naselli,* Palermo, 1755.

Giovanni Meli, *La Bucolica e le Favole morali,* Palermo.

Giuseppe Pitrè, *Biblioteca delle tradizioni popolari siciliane,* Palermo, 1867.

G. Scarcella, *La Sicilia,* Ed. B.&B., Brugherio (MI), 1997.

Mack Smith, *Storia della Sicilia Medievale,* Ed. Laterza, Bari.

V. Titone, *La Sicilia dalla dominazione spagnola all'Unità d'Italia,* Ed. Zanichelli, Bologna, 1955.

V. Titone, *Politica e civiltà.*

Paolo Toschi, *Il folklore,* Ed. S.E.S.A., Bergamo, 1951.

P. Traina Mariano, *Valle del Belice,* Tip. Fiamma Serafica, Palermo.

R. Villari, *Il Sud nella storia d'Italia,* Ed. Laterza, Bari.

~~~~~~ **End of Translation** ~~~~~~

Authors Christine R. Anderson and Ross Todaro, Jr.
thank you for directing your questions, corrections,
or new pertinent information to us
as we continue to keep our Poggioreale research
accurate, alive and growing.

Contact us through our website,
poggiorealeinamerica.com

Made in the USA
Columbia, SC
04 February 2025

e26fe73a-c739-47e6-a135-874d5e3af5c8R01